# FINER THAN HAIR ON A FROG

## More Yarns about Loggers and the Like

Brent A. Connelly

Best wishes!

Brent Connelly

Published by

GENERAL STORE
PUBLISHING HOUSE

499 O'Brien Rd., Box 415
Renfrew, Ontario, Canada K7V 4A6
Telephone (613) 432-7697 or 1-800-465-6072
www.gsph.com

ISBN 978-1-897113-89-9
Printed and Bound in Canada

Cover design and formatting by Robyn Hader
Printing by Custom Printers of Renfrew Ltd.



**Library and Archives Canada Cataloguing in Publication**

Connelly, Brent A., 1939-
Finer than hair on a frog : more yarns about loggers and the like / Brent Connelly.

ISBN 978-1-897113-89-9

1. Logging--Ontario--Algonquin Provincial Park--History--Anecdotes.
2. Loggers--Ontario--Algonquin Provincial Park--History--Anecdotes.
3. Connelly, Brent A., 1939-. 4. Foresters--Ontario--Algonquin Provincial Park--Biography. I. Title.

FC3065.A65C663 2007 634.9'809713147 C2007-906289-X

*This book is dedicated to the loving memory of my parents,*
*George and Marion Connelly, of Brownsburg, Quebec,*
*from a grateful son, and to the memory of*
*my brother-in-law and good friend, Kenneth N. MacTavish.*

# Table of Contents

# Acknowledgements

To properly thank the people who have helped me complete this book may be as challenging as writing the book itself. An attempt to identify them all here would risk omitting at least one. For that reason, I'll strive to extend my thanks at a more personal level.

Once again, my wonderful wife, Heather, was at my side with her usual strong encouragement and occasional advice about General Store Publishing House's senior editor, Susan Code McDougall: "Whatever you do, Brent, listen to Susan. She's a genius." And she is.

At one point in the original manuscript, Susan told me that I was lost in the bush. There is no doubt that if I have made it out of the wilderness, it is because she reminded me how to use my compass one more time.

For the second time, I would like to express my appreciation to publisher Tim Gordon and the staff of General Store Publishing for publishing this book. They are truly a fine group of professionals.

Finally, I have three friends to thank for some amazing stories about loggers. When I called on Tony Vorlicek, Davis MacVicar, and Charlie Downing to share some of their own experiences, they responded with abundance and enthusiasm, as all good storytellers do. Once again, the old story bin spilled over.

# Introduction

***"I mind the time I was snowshoeing through some timber in an area north of Splashy Lake when I came across an albino bull moose. I would have run right into the potlucker, if I hadn't spotted his red tail flashing in the sun."***

—A bunkhouse yarn

In thirty-eight years of working and sitting around lunch fires sharing mugs of tea with loggers in Ontario's Algonquin and Lake Superior Parks, I have had the good fortune of hearing and watching some wonderfully entertaining stories unfold. Any fears that I had about staying active when I retired as a professional forester in 2000 were quickly cast aside with the decision to write a book in an attempt to gather up and share some of these stories with others.

So, *Holy Old Whistlin'—Yarns about Algonquin Park Loggers* was published by General Store Publishing House in November of 2005. I like to think of it as a working man's book—the kind of book that strikes a chord with loggers and their wives and families, who know what it is like to roll out of bed long before the neighbour's rooster has had a chance to clear his throat to announce the new day.

While a mud-caked pickup truck warms up in the driveway, a lunch pail is filled with thick meat loaf sandwiches, topped off with homemade dill pickles and butter tarts as large as soup bowls. A thermos filled with piping-hot coffee finds a precarious resting place on top of the dash of the truck, to provide the sleepy-eyed driver with a few gulps during the long trip into the bush.

A clean shave would have to wait until after supper that night, if there was time. If not, there would be an opportunity before church on Sunday morning. And if there happened to be a snow storm during the day, the kids, upon arriving home from school, would head right to the shed to fire up the snow blower.

Well, *Holy Old Whistlin'* has now become much more than a book for me. It was a door opening onto an exciting world of new experiences, renewed and newly found friendships and, of course, more stories about loggers and the like.

I have often been asked by friends if there would be a sequel to *Holy Old Whistlin'*. The reply was always an easy one: "Not a chance. My story bin is empty—there is nothing more to tell."

Then a funny thing happened. It was a slow day this past spring and my wife, Heather, and I were in between a morning bike ride along the Rideau Canal and a twilight baseball game at Ottawa's Lynx Stadium. With little to do in the meantime, I sat down in the living room and spotted our copy of *Holy Old Whistlin'* sitting on the coffee table.

I picked up the book, and after leafing through a few pages, quickly shook my head with the startling discovery that, although I had written the book, I had never read it. That might sound ridiculous to some, but it is true. I had focused on various sections of the manuscript, but had not taken the time to read the published version from cover to cover. Something like baking a cake and giving it to somebody else to taste.

I have since thought, wouldn't it be fun when next meeting a first-time author to say, "Oh, so you have written a book. Congratulations. But have you read your book? If so, how did you like it?"

So I began reading *Holy Old Whistlin'* and couldn't put the damned thing down. Upon arriving home from the baseball game that night, which, by the way, went into extra innings, I finished reading the book in bed at about the same time some of my logger friends were pulling on a pair of pants and lacing up their boots for another gruelling day in the bush.

As I scanned through the book, it occurred to me that there were still some stories in the bottom of the bin after all. I had heard some new ones in addition to having initially set aside some classics because they didn't fit with the focus of *Holy Old Whistlin'*, which was the loggers of Algonquin Park. And there were stories I had either missed or had forgotten about altogether.

It is my hope that *Finer than Hair on a Frog—More Stories about Loggers and the Like* will do service to some of the rugged loggers I worked with in the Algoma Region of northern Ontario, as well as expand upon the incredible culture of the lumbermen and loggers of Algonquin Park. Reference to the *Like* is to introduce you to some of the other hard-working country folks I have met along the way. There is also some personal stuff with links to logging and working on the land.

To provide some perspective, the following is a brief outline of my forestry career. It began at Rock Lake in Algonquin Park in 1962 with McRae Lumber Company of Whitney, Ontario. In 1965, I moved to Sault Ste. Marie, Ontario, to work for nine years with Weyerhaeuser Canada Ltd. in Lake Superior Park and other parts of Algoma. I was also with Weyerhaeuser in Mattawa, Ontario, for another year (1970) working in Algonquin Park and the Upper Ottawa Valley. In 1975, I was hired by the newly established Ontario Crown agency, the Algonquin Forestry Authority (AFA), which was established to manage the forests of Algonquin Park. I remained with the AFA for twenty-five years until my retirement in 2000.

What a wonderful feeling it is to be able to say that I have had the privilege of working for thirty-eight years in two of Ontario's premier provincial parks.

So, pull the plug on the TV or computer, steep a pot of tea, put up your feet and meet some more wonderful loggers and the like.

But before you do, once again I have buried something in this book which I challenge the reader to find. This time it is a made-up term and not an outrageous description of a logging tool as hidden in *Holy Old Whistlin'*. And the offer to the discoverer remains unchanged, except for location; I will treat the first one to find the bogus term to a genuine bush lunch on the shores of Huff and Puff Lake. (To date, ten people have contacted me after having found the logging tool in *Holy Old Whistlin'*. The first one to do so was Don Wallace of Pembroke. If I hear from another dozen or so maybe we could justify hiring a bus and make the outing really worthwhile, topping off the baloney and sardine sandwiches with some tales, tall tales, and maybe even a lie or two.)

PART I

# ALGONQUIN PARK AND THEREABOUTS

# Chapter 1: Do Potatoes Grow in Algonquin Park?

*"The loggers of Algonquin Park wear big boots but leave soft footprints."*
—Carl Corbett, General Manager, Algonquin Forestry Authority

Well, isn't that a ridiculous notion? It's unlikely that a single potato plant grows on the landscape of modern-day Algonquin Park. However, such was not always the case. During the busy squared timber days of the last half of the 1800s, resourceful entrepreneurs running logging depots and "stop-over" facilities raised their own hogs and chickens, and grew bushels of potatoes and other vegetables in the hostile soil of a forested land. The hard-working loggers who worked like beavers along the waterways of Algonquin bringing vital timber to a developing nation had to be well fed.

However, this chapter is not really about potatoes at all. It's about loggers and lumbermen. But anybody who has ever dug a hill of potatoes can make the connection. A hill of potatoes always has one or two eager spuds breaking through the surface with innocent little eyes peeking at the sky. As the hoe flicks the side of the hill, out rolls a family of huge golden nuggets, a smack-of-the-lips away from a ladle of steaming-hot roast beef gravy.

That is what I have discovered about these stories of loggers. Just below the surface there are always more of the same, ready for the stroke of a hoe. It's for that reason that, whenever possible, I like to take a nostalgia trip back to the communities around Algonquin Park to talk to old friends and meet new ones. One such trip was on a cold fall day when Heather and I loaded up the cooler with sandwiches and headed to Barry's Bay, Madawaska and Whitney, all located not far from the southeastern boundary of Algonquin Park.

Our first stop was to meet retired trucker Harold Griffith in Madawaska. Harold and his wife, Jessie, were waiting for us at their kitchen table, which was piled high with albums containing faded, old-time logging photos. A steeping pot of tea was sitting invitingly in the middle.

Harold is a slight man in his late seventies with the steady eye of a truck driver. His friendly grin opened the door onto a wonderful couple of hours of stepping back in time and listening to his remarkable outlook on life.

"Yes, sir," he began, "out in my back shed I have a three-year supply of dry, split firewood and a barrel of coal oil. Those Hydro guys can bring on the blackouts, and Jessie and me won't skip a beat. If there is no TV to watch, we'll just get out the old cribbage board and light up a lamp. Maybe, we'll just have to go to bed a little earlier at night," he added with a twinkle in his eye.

Harold Griffith "outbacka" his place in Madawaska, Ontario: "Life is good when the woodshed is full."

We talked about J. S. L. "Jack" McRae, the well-known lumber baron and owner of McRae Lumber Company of Whitney. Harold had driven log trucks for McRae many years and knew him well. I also had worked for Jack McRae at his Rock Lake sawmill operation in Algonquin Park. I had been a naïve rookie forester starting my first job in a man's world and admired and learned much from Jack McRae. He was a very successful, crusty old lumberman with a hard-nosed management style that would make modern corporate consultants shake their heads in disbelief. I also worked for his equally capable son, Donald. I like to think that they both mentored me well.

Jack McRae, or The Boss as all his men called him, was known to fly into a fit of rage whenever things were not going well. There is a story about him that Harold and I were both familiar with. One winter during a period of freezing rain, The Boss was visiting one of his logging camps and threw a big table-model radio out of the camp office window when the weather forecast called for more of the same misery.

With excitement in his voice, Harold elaborated, "I was in the camp at Hay Lake that night about sixty years ago. There had been a couple of days of freezing rain, and it looked like there was more to come. In the meantime, the log haul had been shut down. The only thing us truckers could do was sit around the bunkhouse, play poker, and eat McRae's five-star grub. The old lad could see our idleness and it put him in an ugly mood.

"We were sitting in the bunkhouse waiting for the supper bell to go in the cookery, and when it rang, we started walking down the path past the office. All of a sudden there was the sound of broken glass, and an old wooden radio came flying out the front window. It damned near hit me on the head. And right behind the radio stomped The Boss kicking it to smithereens as he walked to supper. The snowbanks along the path were strewn with pieces of the radio right down to the cookery step. It's a good thing that we didn't have televisions in those days or he might have wiped out his whole crew.

"And throughout supper, all we could hear was The Boss growling as he ate his T-bone steak, 'The only thing I'm doing in the goddamned lumber business these days is making debt.'"

Harold went on to describe another classic tale about Jack McRae. Up until about 1950, logging operators hauled logs with dual-wheeled, single-axle trucks. Since they were lightly constructed vehicles, they were unable to haul heavy loads and were costly to maintain. Then along came the revolutionary tandem truck in the early fifties. These heavier-duty trucks had improved traction on bush roads, reduced maintenance costs, and hauled substantially increased payloads. Jack McRae had his shrewd eye on this promising new development.

Harold's father was in the trucking business and had been one of the first in the country to purchase a new tandem truck. At the time, Harold was driving a truck for McRae's out of the Hay Lake camp. He tells of a meeting with Jack McRae one night in the camp.

"I was relaxing in the bunkhouse one night after supper when another truck driver came in the front door and said to me with a serious look on his face, 'Harold, The Boss wants to see you in the office right away.'

"Holy Jeez, I thought. The old bugger is going to fire me for something. Can't figure out why, though. Every morning I'm in my truck and heading to the bush for my first load before the cook has had a chance to put his teeth in and think about making breakfast. Maybe it's because he overheard me laughing like a son of a bitch that night he kicked the tubes out of the radio.

"He was waiting for me sitting on a chair when I opened the door into the office. He didn't say hello, gidday, or ask me how the log haul was going—not a word. As he lit up a cigarette, he motioned for me to sit down on a nearby chair. He leaned over, put his two elbows on the table, and looked me squarely in the eyes.

"'Harold,' he said, 'now tell me about those goddamned tandems.'"

Then it was off to Whitney, a village of about 900 proud citizens, many of them of Polish descent. I had lived in Whitney for close to three years and had many happy memories of that peaceful little community situated at the point where Galeairy Lake flows into the Madawaska River.

Retired logger, Fred Kmith, greeted us in a quaint little workshop behind his home on the top of the hill overlooking Whitney. Fred is a quiet man with a wonderful sense of humour. I couldn't even take a wild guess at his age, except to say that if he is seventy-five or older, he looks fifteen years younger than what he actually is. He stands straight and is physically fit from years of working as a logger.

He was crafting some miniature rocking chairs and salad spoons, and insisted on giving Heather one of each. The walls of Fred's shop were still adorned with his famous collection of antique axes, including the renowned two-man axe. The one thing that I hadn't noticed on a previous visit was a bell tower on the roof of his shop, connected to a rope that hung down on the inside of the building. Before we left to go into the kitchen to have a cup of tea and a piece of Polish fruitcake with his wife Norma, Fred had me pull the rope.

The result was a loud ringing sound which echoed throughout the valley below, probably only matched by the chime of the one in the huge Catholic church towering over the town on a nearby hill. It occurred to me afterwards that this was probably Fred's way of announcing the arrival of another curious visitor to his museum.

As we enjoyed our tea and fruitcake, Fred told us the story of his bell, which had been given to him by his old friend, Raymond Bernaskie.

The Paugh Lake road leads northerly from Barry's Bay towards Algonquin Park. It is the only access to a gentle countryside sprinkled with happy homes and small farms. It was here, sometime in the early 1930s, that we learn of the first known origin of the bell.

As a young boy, Raymond Bernaskie attended a small one-room school along the road. The bell was mounted on its roof. A young female teacher was faced with the challenge of teaching several grades at the same time, with some of her students probably being close to her own age, or maybe even older. To maintain control and order, she took full advantage of the bell and used it with a youthful zeal. It rang constantly throughout the school day, and for the students, it seemed that the damned thing was ringing much too often. They were becoming weary of it.

One Halloween night, Raymond and a few of his chums decided to put an end to it all. It was time for that old bell to go. So, after dark, they climbed up onto the roof and released the tired bell from its years of captivity. The bell was rolled down off the roof. And then the fun and the hard work began.

The bell weighed over a hundred pounds, so the young lads had their newly discovered strength fully tested as they struggled to muscle the bell into the bush, as far away from the school as their skinny little bodies could drag it. They left it there covered over with brush so that it could not be seen from an adjacent field.

The next morning in front of smiling students, the teacher walked to the rope which had not been removed and was still dangling from the ceiling. She pulled on the rope to announce the beginning of classes. A strange silence fell on the school as the empty rope fell limply to the floor.

Fred Kmith, Whitney, Ontario, presiding over his axe museum and the old Paugh Lake school bell: "Let's all meet at Fred's place next Halloween night to ring the bell."

That night at an emergency meeting of the school trustees and a few parents, nobody came forward to shed any light on the whereabouts of the bell. And so, there was nothing to do but give the teacher a worn-out old cow bell that had rested for the previous decade on a shelf in a nearby barn.

Shortly after the bell incident, the school was closed permanently and the students were moved to another school. And life carried on along the Paugh Lake road.

Many years went by and the memory of that old bell faded, until one day when Raymond Bernaskie, who had just returned from serving overseas in World War II, went for a walk in the bush for a relaxing partridge hunt. He walked into the overgrown area where the school had once stood. "I wonder if that old bell is still around," he thought.

It took him awhile, but eventually he found it in the same place, but now barely visible under the new growth of trees and underbrush. Raymond could hardly contain himself he was so excited. He walked to a neighbouring farm and asked the farmer to pull it out to a nearby road with his horse where he picked it up and took it home. It remained on Raymond's back porch for four or five years until one day Raymond's wife told him in no uncertain terms, "Raymond, I wish you would get that old bell out of here. Every time I go out to hang the clothes on the line, I trip over the darned thing."

At that time, Raymond was working in the bush for McRae Lumber Company and was staying in a camp near Opeongo Lake in Algonquin Park. He thought that the cook in the camp would like to have it mounted on the cookery to ring the men in for their meals. But there already was a steel triangle hanging at the front door of the cookery, which the cookee used to hit with a steel rod at mealtime. It did the job, and the bell wasn't needed, so it sat on the ground outside the cookery for another couple of years.

Fred was also working out of the same camp at that time and happened to notice the bell one day. He asked a few questions and found out that it belonged to Raymond. When asked about it, Raymond was quite happy to give it to his friend, knowing that now it would have a good home. One day, Raymond helped Fred load it into the trunk of his car and Fred took it home where it laid out behind his house for about ten years.

Then, in the middle of a pitch-black night, Fred awakened with a start and a sudden realization: "Damn it all to hell, I have to do something about that old bell." Before he went back to sleep that night he vowed to make it his first priority in the morning. Right after breakfast, he fetched the bell and took it to John Mastine who was the maintenance superintendent for McRae Lumber in Whitney. John welded an arm onto the small end of the bell, and a bearing with a grease nipple was fitted to the bell.

Fred sanded and painted the bell silver and cut a hole in the roof of his workshop. With the help of another old friend, Dave Harper, the bell was then raised onto the roof. A bell tower with a removable roof was constructed over the bell. Now, whenever the bell is overworked and starts to squeak, Fred can reach in with his grease gun and give it a shot of grease.

When I asked Fred if it was used much, he replied, "In the beginning, the kids came around to give the rope a pull to hear the bell ring, but now it's just an ornament. However, every year on Halloween night, I go out into the shop and ring it for awhile. Seems like the proper thing to do."

So, there you have it. About seventy years in the life of an old school bell. Wouldn't it be nice if we knew when and where it was born and what brought it to that little schoolhouse along the Paugh Lake road in the first place. Maybe on some dark night in the future, a Halloween ghost will come by Fred's place with the answer.

After we left Fred and Norma, the next visit was to Elva Gorgerat's Twin "E" confectionery shop, which she operates with her husband, Ernie. It is near the Highway 60 bridge over the Madawaska River in downtown Whitney and can be anything you want it to be—a confectionery, lunch bar, lottery outlet, or just a fun place to pass the time. It is a place where local, national, and international news is available in printed form or straight from the horse's mouth, quite frequently prefaced with the old expression, "somebody told somebody."

To many, it's Whitney's equivalent of a Tim Hortons or the town's welcome centre with a large coffee urn sitting on the end of the counter near a few tables covered with clear plastic. A styrofoam cup sits near the coffee pot and patrons drop fifty cents in it, as they help themselves to a cup while lighting or rolling a cigarette. A no-smoking zone is still in the conceptual stage at the Twin "E".

It was a cold, dismal day, the kind when frowns outpace smiles in most places. But not at Elva's.

The tinkling of a small bell from the top of the door announced our arrival. Elva was behind the counter selling a can of Copenhagen snuff to a little old lady. She never did say if the snuff was for the little old lady or for somebody at home. (I knew a logger once who, instead of pepper, would sprinkle a little snuff over his sunny-side-up eggs in the morning. "Best way I know of to get a run at the day," he would boast.)

"How are you today, Elva?" I asked.

Without hesitation, she looked me straight in the eye and replied with a huge grin, "I'm finer than hair on a frog."

It seems to me that no matter what the weather is or the circumstances are, you know that you are having a good day when you are greeted by somebody who tells you that they are finer than hair on a frog.

I have it all staged in my mind: the next time we are invited to a formal, upscale cocktail party in Ottawa and are approached by an uppercruster wearing Gucci shoes and an ascot, with his little pinky curled around the stem of a martini glass, who asks, without giving a hoot one way or another, "How are you today?" I will reply, with the widest smile I can muster, "I'm finer than hair on a frog. How about you?" That will spin him in his tracks. I can hardly wait.

We sat down with a cup of coffee and chatted with Elva, Ernie, and three old lads wearing baseball caps huddled at a corner table. A friendly young parish priest came in to buy a newspaper and stayed for a few minutes to talk with us. Shortly after the 3:00 p.m. shift change in McRae's sawmill, a few mill workers arrived for a coffee and a chat, coming through the door, busily brushing sawdust from their eyebrows and clothes.

The sight reminded me of another time when I was working for Weyerhaeuser on logging operations north of Sault Ste. Marie. Loggers and truckers would stop occasionally for coffee at the Lighthouse Restaurant along Highway 17.

The friendly proprietor, Beryle Ogden, could often be overheard saying, "Here come those damn loggers again; they stop in for a twenty-five-cent cup of coffee and leave a dollar's worth of mud on the floor."

Early the next morning we were at Elva's for breakfast, one that would match any I have enjoyed in logging camps over the years. We each received a heaping hot plate of eggs, home fries, bacon and, believe it or not, four pieces of Texas toast with enough jam to feed a dozen kids. When I offered a surplus piece of toast to a couple of fellows at the next table, they nodded quietly, "No thanks." They had eaten before us and were probably already looking forward to their lunch by that time.

When I complimented Elva on the nice thick bacon she had prepared, she replied, "Working men like thick bacon, and I order it sliced that way. Wouldn't feed my cat that see-through shit that you guys in the city get at Loblaws."

That morning we decided to drive into Algonquin to see the park's Logging Museum and Visitors' Centre, two magnificent facilities that all Ontario taxpayers should be proud of and plan to visit sometime. As we rounded a curve on Highway 60 near the Rock Lake turn, I had to brake quickly and pull over to the side of the road. Straddling the white line stood a huge bull moose shaking his head at us while defiantly standing guard for the moose nation of Algonquin Park. The sight of the moose flashed me back to another story about two other lumbermen I had done business and become friends with during my time working for the AFA.

Johnnie Shaw and his brother Donald operated the Herb Shaw & Sons Ltd. sawmilling and utility pole manufacturing facility in Pembroke. They formed a tag-team match well respected in the lumber business throughout eastern Ontario. Johnnie, the quiet, shy one, was president of the company and the elder of the two. He was easily recognized with his customary cigarette, high-top work boots, light blue shirt and khaki work pants, the cuffs of which served as ashtrays in no-smoking zones. Donald was the garrulous one with a big grin underwriting the ever-present designer sunglasses and loosely knotted Mike Hammer tie. Both could be tough and profane or smooth and charming, depending on whether they were buying defective logs or selling high-quality lumber. However, at no time in any of their transactions were the dollar signs very far out of their sight.

One time, Johnnie and Donald needed to buy a large front-end loader for use in their pole yard and had heard about an equipment auction south of Rouyn-Noranda, Quebec. They decided to drive up to check on what was available.

It was a long drive, so they left Pembroke early in the morning, crossing into Quebec at Temiscaming. These were not men given to spending an evening sipping cognac and lounging in a hot tub in a northern Quebec hotel. Not a chance. There was work to do around the mill or in the bush the next day, so they would return home late that night.

Sadly, and without their knowledge, there was a major bank robbery in Temiscaming that day. Shots were fired and one or more bank employees was injured. There may even have been a fatality—I don't recall the details.

On the way home after dark that night, with Johnnie's fuzz-buster fully engaged, they struck a bull moose on a desolate section of the highway north of Temiscaming. The moose was knocked down, but not killed and, of course, the front of Johnnie's truck was banged up somewhat, but still mobile.

The moose was not able to get to his feet, so they decided he would have to be put out of his misery. Since they didn't have a rifle with them, they grabbed an axe from behind the seat and approached the moose. Suddenly, the poor animal cleared his head and jumped to his feet, running into the bush with Johnnie and Donald hot on his trail. They ran for a few minutes through the blood-soaked underbrush, but finally gave up the chase after the moose disappeared into the blackness of the dense bush.

It had been a long day, it was late, and they were tired and hungry. When they limped into Temiscaming, with one dead headlight hanging by a wire over the bumper and the other aiming up at the moon, Johnnie steered his battered truck into the parking lot of a roadside restaurant. They didn't pay too much attention to the six Sûreté du Québec cruisers parked near the restaurant.

With their clothes splattered with moose blood from head to toe, they sat down in a booth. Several police officers were sitting around a large table at the other end of the restaurant and had not seen them come in.

Donald, who had previously only visited Quebec for the occasional stag party or shivaree, asked the frightened, wide-eyed waitress in his faltering French, "*Comment ça va* . . . what in hell are all the cops doing in here? Is it poker night in Temiscaming?" It was only then that they were told about the bank robbery that day. The robbers were still on the loose and the cops had the dragnet out.

As he parked a huge wad of gum on his left ear, hitched up his pants, and cleared his throat, Johnnie summed up the experience to me: "Hrrmmm . . . As I looked down at the moose blood on my pant legs, I said to Donald, 'Let's get the hell out of here.' And we ran out the back door right past the cook in the kitchen, still chewing on our goddamned pepper steaks."

As we were pulled over on the side of the road to take a picture of the moose, I was reminded of another time that I had stopped my truck alongside a highway, but for a much different reason.

Hec Clouthier Sr. from Pembroke ran his own logging business for many years and, along with three of his sons, operated a bush camp on the Brent Road which led into Algonquin Park from Highway 17 between Deep River and Mattawa. He was short in stature, but tall in feistiness and determination to "Git 'er done." Leading up to his passing in 2003, Hec's constant companion was his faithful canine, Freckles. I have a wonderful photograph given to me by Hec's son, Tommy. It shows Hec and Freckles sitting side-by-side in the end of a boat fishing on a lake—a weathered working-man's hand sharing the outboard motor controls with a warm paw.

One summer evening after a long day of working in the Kiosk area of Algonquin Park, I was driving home alone to Pembroke. A few miles east of Mattawa, I noticed that I was being tailgated by a huge, black New

Yorker sedan. In the rear-view mirror, the driver appeared to be a short man, while a larger figure sat in the passenger's seat. In a few minutes, the car began flashing its headlights.

I pulled over to the side of the road expecting that there was something wrong with my truck. The car also stopped, and as I walked back to talk to the driver, I found old Hec boasting a huge smile. Beside him sitting upright on a pile of pillows from Hec's bunkhouse was Freckles enjoying the countryside scenery. He looked like a noble Duke of Edinburgh riding in a golden chariot and waving to the throngs.

I jokingly asked Hec if he had Freckles belted in. "No," he said with a grin. "I only tried to put a seat belt on him once. That was the first and the last time that he ever growled at me."

Hec and Freckles were planning on spending the night at his logging camp, which was a few miles down the road. "Why don't you stop in for a toddy on your way home, Brent?" he invited. And I did.

The first toddy was followed by a second, then by a third, which was followed by a phone call to Heather. "I'm having a sleepover at Hec's place. I'll see you tomorrow."

Hec and I solved many of the world's problems that night. It's too bad that old Freckles, who lay quietly with his eyes wide open all evening at our feet, was the only one to have the benefit of our wisdom.

There is one thing I could count on over the years. Whenever visiting somebody in Whitney, you could always count on leaving with a huge smile on your face and a warm feeling in your heart. A visit with Isadore (Bob) Shalla, an old logger I had worked with at McRae Lumber Co.'s operation at Rock Lake was a perfect example of that.

I hadn't seen him in forty-one years when I pulled into the yard of his little house overlooking the OPP station in Whitney and found him on his back with two legs sticking out from underneath a maroon station wagon. Here was a man well into his eighties, whose gnarled hands told of a lifetime of hard work, changing the oil in his car, a million miles and years away from the manor in Barry's Bay. Who needs Canadian Tire when you have a wrench and a case of oil in the basement? (If you drive around Whitney and look closely enough, there are many backyard ramps where resourceful men, and maybe even some women, do their own mechanical work.)

As I looked down at Bob and introduced myself, he jumped up as straight and lean as he had ever been, and looked at me with a puzzled look on his face. "Holy jumping, Brent," he exclaimed. "You were just a young lad the last time I saw you. Now you are an old bugger, just like me. I wouldn't have recognized you if I had met you in my soup." We chatted for awhile and shared a chuckle about his older brother, Frank, who was also a logger and commonly added a thimble of brandy to a fresh can of snuff.

There is another thing I have discovered about Whitney. If you wait around long enough in one spot, somebody else is sure to come along for a visit. Sure enough, a few minutes later, a pickup truck pulled into Bob's yard. It was his neighbour, Florian Kuiack, a big, jovial man with a wide grin overtopping a chin or two. (People grin a lot in Whitney. I guess it's because life is good there.)

"You know, Brent," Florian said, "there has been quite a bit of chatter around town lately about Fred Kmith's two-man axe. But that's nothing compared to what I heard from an old logger years ago. He told me that he had worked for J. R. Booth in the bush up north of Opeongo Lake in the Park back in the thirties and that the white pine trees were so big that they had to fell them with three-man crosscut saws. Now wouldn't that be a terror to behold? The way I figured it worked was that there were two gigantic men at each end of the saw and another bull of a man to drag it from tree to tree."

"Makes sense to me, Florian," Bob chipped in with a chuckle, "especially the bull part."

If you drive through communities like Barry's Bay, Whitney, Pembroke, or Mattawa between 4:00 a.m. and 5:00 a.m. on any weekday you will see them: kitchen lights glowing through the darkness, a logger gulping one last cup of coffee while a bleary-eyed wife wearing a housecoat shuffles around in the background trying to jam a fifth baloney sandwich into an overfilled lunch box. Loggers, truckers, and farmers and their families get up early in the morning and have little use for late-risers. If you want to sleep beyond daybreak, move to the city.

Henry Elis was an early-riser and for many years worked long hours owning and operating a road construction and maintenance business in the Algonquin region. Apart from being one of the good guys, he was also a skilled equipment operator. His brother-in-law, Harvey Reckzin, who worked with Henry for many years, once told me that Henry could pick an olive out of a martini with the bucket of his excavator in a blinding blizzard.

In September 2005, Henry lost a courageous battle with cancer. To celebrate his life, Heather and I attended a graveside ceremony in a beautiful little Lutheran cemetery on top of a hill overlooking the Lake Dore Road near Golden Lake village. There were many loggers in attendance, some of whom I had not seen in years. One of them was logging contractor John Jeffreys from Barry's Bay.

As John and I chatted, we had a chuckle about an experience we had shared with another logging contractor, Walter Dombroski, also of Barry's Bay. At the time, John worked as a logging foreman for Walter, who was a major contractor for the Algonquin Forestry Authority in Algonquin Park. I was working for the AFA out of the Pembroke office and was responsible for the Dombroski operation.

Walter was another one of those loggers who took pride in jumping out of bed well before breakfast each morning. He had no tolerance for late-risers and over the years we teased each other over the matter. He claimed that since I was frequently office-bound that I worked bankers hours.

It was in late March one year when Walter, John, and I had planned a snowmobile trip into a remote area of the park north of the Basin Depot Road. We wanted to take a look at an area to be logged by the Dombroski operation the following year. Since the deep snow would begin to melt by midday, it was necessary to travel early in the morning to take advantage of the crust. Otherwise, the snow machines would sink in the snow making it very difficult to travel. Getting stuck fifteen miles from our trucks was a scary thought, especially since snowshoeing out to the main road would be out of the question.

We had arranged to meet one morning at 4:30 in John's driveway on the Airport Road near Barry's Bay. The previous week, AFA's area forester, Bob Pick, had wrecked our only snowmachine by taking a bank shot off a huge yellow birch tree, so I had a forty-five minute drive from Pembroke to Barry's Bay that morning to pick up a borrowed one from Dombroski. Walter lived just down the road from John, about five minutes away.

I can remember thinking the night before that the old bugger was not going to get the best of me. I would be in John's driveway trimming up his snowbanks with a shovel when Walter arrived. That'd keep him quiet.

Well, so much for my plan. I went to bed that night with my clothes on and left Pembroke shortly after the late show had finished. When I pulled into John's driveway, I could see John and Walter peering out the window at my headlights, waving their coffee cups at me.

"What in hell kept you?" Walter growled as his big red moustache twitched. "We just finished our second pot of coffee. The day is half shot now. Good thing I have a big lunch. Looks like we'll be spending the night in the bush."

It was on a bitterly cold January afternoon that Heather and I stopped in to visit Francis Conway in Barry's Bay. Francis, who shows a strong physical resemblance to his well-known son, Sean, a former MPP for the area and minister of education for Ontario, was in his late eighties at the time of our visit and lived by himself in his home near the centre of town.

As I approached the back door, I could see him sitting at the kitchen table watching a small TV through a fog of cigarette smoke. (Jim Hickey of Deep River told me once that for as long as he had known Francis, he faithfully quit smoking each year for Lent.)

He greeted Heather and me warmly, quickly inviting us inside. A tall, thin, soft-spoken man with a friendly face, he stood straight as a poker as he smartly manoeuvred a walker to escort us through the dining room into the tidy living room for our chat. He had just returned from having hip surgery and was quick to point out that the walker would only be needed for another day or two. After that, it would be put out in the garage or passed on to some feeble old friend who really needed it.

His home buzzed with activity: a neighbour came in with a couple of menu choices for the dinner she would bring over to him later on; another neighbour showed up with his snowblower to clean out the driveway; a grandson came in looking forward to spending the afternoon with his grandfather—maybe it would be a game of cards or a story or two.

Francis was well-known in the Ottawa Valley as a master saw-filer and had worked in sawmills for various lumber companies throughout his career. (The two key men in the efficient operation of a sawmill were the head sawyer and the saw-filer.) He was highly skilled in his trade and had been very much in demand, having worked many years for Murray Bros. Lumber Company of Madawaska and Ben Hokum & Son Ltd. of Killaloe. He had also worked for McRae Lumber at Rock Lake for a short time.

I had never met Francis in person before and had only talked to him once over the telephone when he told me the story about Jack McRae asking a Whitney priest to say a prayer for his son, Donald, who was in a German POW camp at the time. "And pray like a son of a bitch," was The Boss's request of the priest.

It turned out, much to the surprise of both of us, that he had worked for Weyerhaeuser Canada Ltd.'s Mattawa operation the same time that I worked there. He filed saws in their Big Jocko River sawmill, and since I was involved in the logging operations, our paths didn't cross.

However, we were both there on a cold winter night when the Jocko sawmill burned to the ground. As we talked about that experience, we shared the same feeling of sadness as we saw jobs and dreams go up in smoke. It wasn't long after the fire that Weyerhaeuser shut down their entire Mattawa operation, placing a dark cloud over the future of a couple hundred families in Mattawa and surrounding communities.

What an enjoyable afternoon it was as we shared stories about Mattawa and other places where we had worked.

One of my favourites, as told by Francis, was of a lumberman he once worked for. One day the fellow came running through the filing room where Francis was working and ran down a set of stairs leading to the lower level of the sawmill. A few minutes later, he stomped up the stairs and raced through the filing room into another part of the mill. In about ten minutes, he was back again, streaking through the filing room and running down the stairs one more time.

Francis was puzzled and when the guy came back up the stairs for the second time, he shouted over the noise of screaming saws, "Are you looking for somebody?"

"Goddamned, if I know," was the slurred reply, "I'm drunk."

My nostalgic glimpse back at the wonderful stories and memories of living in Whitney and working for McRae Lumber Co. in Algonquin Park wound down for me in May of 2006, when I attended the wake for Donald McRae, who had lived all his life in Whitney until he passed away in the Barry's Bay hospital at the age of ninety. It was then that I learned more about the man I had worked for forty years before. He had not shared his POW experience with me, so I had little knowledge of the sacrifice that he had made. It was only through talking to his family that day did I realize what a hero I had been privileged to know.

His daughter, Janet Webber, described Donald's wartime experience further in an excerpt about his life featured in the May 24, 2006, edition of *The Eganville Leader*.

> Once WWII broke out my father joined the military in 1941 serving with the RCAF in Europe.
>
> An aerial gunner assigned with the RAF 102 squadron, Mr. McRae was subsequently shot down in June 1942 while on a bombing run. After parachuting to safety with their plane ablaze over the German–Dutch border, Mr. McRae was taken prisoner, spending 33 months as a POW, primarily in the camp at Stagan.
>
> He spent most of his 33 months at the camp at Stagan which is noted in history as the site of the great escape. He wasn't involved in the escape per se, partly because he and others were transferred on suspicion of being involved with something just before it.

"He had been involved with digging the tunnels, but because he was a larger man he didn't actually do the digging," she added. "He worked the bellows to supply air to those who were digging."

There was sadness that day in the little A-frame United Church on the side of the hill in Whitney where Donald's funeral was held, but there also was laughter and celebration as those attending traded stories about the two renowned lumbermen that we had all known and respected, Donald McRae and his father Jack McRae.

One such story was told to me by Donald's daughter, Janet. It was about her grandfather.

She had left Whitney to attend university and would occasionally come home for visits. Once, she brought a friend home for a weekend. The friend was a city girl and had not been to Whitney before. They were staying at Janet's grandparents' place in Airy, and at first, she was a little anxious knowing that her grandfather could show a rough edge at times.

However, her fears were alleviated when early the first morning, she awakened to the mouth-watering aroma of bacon and eggs cooking. Janet woke up her friend and the two girls ran downstairs in anticipation of a good old-fashioned lumberjack breakfast.

They were greeted by Janet's grandfather, who was frying up a snack of bacon and eggs for him and his old hound. The dog was hovering over a dinner plate on the floor, licking his chops to the beat of an excited tail thumping against the side of the stove.

"Your grandmother will be down in a few minutes," he said to the girls. "She'll make you some breakfast."

One other time, Janet described coming home excited from high school in Bancroft to announce the news that she had come second in her class at the end of the school year.

"Who came first?" her grandfather questioned stiffly without offering her his congratulations.

The church hall that day was filled with many of Donald McRae's grandchildren, many of whom had not known their great-grandfather, Jack. As one generation fades away, it is sad to think that so do some of the stories of these amazing characters. But on the opposite end are new generations on the horizon. Jamie McRae is the great-grandson of J. S. L. "Jack" McRae and is now working for McRae Lumber Co. in their Whitney mills. Jack McRae was also in the lumber business with his father, John D. McRae of Eganville. That makes Jamie the fifth generation McRae in the lumber business. How is that for human and forest sustainability?

It seems to me that the David Suzukis of the world would quickly have their eyes and hearts opened if they would just take the time to visit people like Jamie McRae, Fred Kmith, and Bob Shalla, or drop in to chat with the lads down at Elva's. They might even be treated to a delicious snack of polish sausage, perogies, and homemade bread. On second thought, maybe it would be a stale bun and a cup of cold tea.

But what makes it all so wonderful is knowing that there will always be new stories to hear, cherished and retold. And forever there will be another hill of potatoes to hoe.

# Chapter 2: Misery Mountain

*"There I was, my truck and tractor both stuck to the axles in that damned old mud hole. Good thing that the wife had taken the car to town or it would be buried in there, too."*

—Unknown farmer, "Inbacka" Lanark

Loggers, foresters, and other bush workers are called upon to drive their pickup trucks on bush roads, which are in some cases barely more than rough trails. Often they drive alone, far from active logging operations, making the risk of getting stuck and staying stuck in a mud hole or washout always a threat. That is why they carry chainsaws, come-alongs, and powerful bumper jacks in their trucks.

Adding to the pressure of getting stuck in a remote area, alone, with no help nearby is the unwritten "code of the bush," which states that under no circumstances should any other person living on the planet hear of one becoming stuck and having to seek help. It is the kiss of death with co-workers and friends given licence to remind the individual about the experience until his dying day.

I am told that if a logger does get stuck he has three choices: he can jack, lever, and pull on his truck, or burl the rear tires until they are smoking and the truck is freed; he can wait until sundown, walk to town, hire a wrecker and bribe the driver to keep his mouth shut; or he can wait with the truck until searchers find his bones.

As I explain this, I need to emphasize that since I have not once been seriously stuck in more than forty years of driving on bush roads, I do not have first-hand knowledge of the "code of the bush." This information only comes to me second-hand, from others who have lived the experience.

One day I received a call from Arnold Johnston, who introduced himself as a farmer from "Inbacka" Lanark. He was anxious to tell me about the farmers' equivalent of the loggers' code of the bush.

Now there is that "Inbacka" thing I am compelled to comment on. So while Arnold patiently stands by with his wonderful story, I would like to take you on a little ramble that has more twists and turns than Tommy Cannon's cinnamon rolls.

Who is Tommy Cannon? He was an old bush camp cook I knew when we both worked for McRae Lumber Co. at Rock Lake. A whiff of his fabulous rolls would rouse a black bear from a deep February slumber.

Once again, I would like to share a long-standing observation that has always amused me while living and working in the Lower and Upper Ottawa Valleys on both the Ontario and Quebec sides, and the Algoma Region of Ontario: many small communities have another place with the same name located in back of it or somewhere nearby. "Inbacka" is the shortened term commonly used. I have a recent example.

For over thirty years during the week preceding Labour Day, Pembroke, Ontario, hosts its annual step-dancing and fiddling competition. The event attracts up to 4,000 people to the pretty little city of 14,500 along the shores of the Ottawa River.

Competitors, both young and old, attend, as well as throngs of smiling folk who love old-time music and dancing. It is much more than a competition. It is a festival abounding with music, dancing, storytelling, friendships, and plain old-fashioned fun. Old grouches are welcomed with open arms and converted to the happy side of life in less time than it takes to tune a fiddle.

Apart from the competition, which is held in Pembroke's Memorial Centre, a centrepiece of the event is Riverside Park, which is renamed Fiddle Park for the week. As many as 1,500 recreational vehicles assemble in the park, transforming it into a busy little city complete with street signs and shuttle bus stops.

As soon as the RVs are parked upon arrival and hooked up to the services, jam sessions sprout up under trailer canopies, and large make-shift tents appear like dandelions exploding through the grass in the spring. And everywhere in Fiddle Park, people can be seen strolling happily from one jam session to another, carrying lawn chairs, fiddle and guitar cases, and tape recorders. Once in awhile, walkers can be seen moving aside to permit a large bass fiddle fitted with an attached wheel or perched on a kid's wagon to be pulled by its proud owner to a performance at the next hot spot.

An aerial view of Fiddle Park, Pembroke, Ontario.

Pembroke's Fiddle Park. The Trailer Park Boys and a girl: Bob Meehan, Ray Harnish, Brent Connelly, Bernie "Bubbles" McCambridge, "The other Johnnie Cash," René Foran, August Boudens, Bob DeJongh, Larry VanLieshout, Ernie McKee, Emily Harnish, Jim Sterling, Bradley Moncion, Ray Brisson. "We're running out of parking space, so we'll just stand your trailer on end or hang it from a tree and try to give you a little bit of hydro and a little bit of water."

For several years, Heather and I have worked as volunteers at Fiddle Park. She helps out in the registration office and I work with the crew which escorts the RVs to their parking spots. Some call us the Trailer Park Boys.

It's a sheer delight to be a part of the friendly banter that goes on between the crew and wide-eyed visitors as they gaze with amazement at a sea of RVs. Bernie "Bubbles" McCambridge was once overheard telling a nervous newcomer he was escorting into the park, "Boy, do I have a treat for you. The honeymoon suite with a river view, and only a stone's throw to the poutine truck."

Minnie LaSalle was once directing the driver of a half-ton truck pulling a trailer. The trailer was purchased a few days before, so the poor guy had only driven it frontwards. He had not had the opportunity to practise his backing-up skills. A cheering crowd gathered as Minnie attempted to help him back into a tight spot.

It was one jackknife after another, with a back-up ahead a bit, and a swing to the right, followed by an allemande left, and a dos-a-dos.

At one point, the excited driver, who was now looking up towards the heavens with raised arms, had lost track of front and back, left and right, as he performed before hundreds of spectators, yelled back at Minnie, "What side is my awning on?"

"It's on the same side it was when you left home this morning," replied a grinning Minnie.

During the 2006 Fiddle Week, I had the pleasure of escorting a young family into the park. The father was driving a large van loaded with an assortment of jovial kids and a smiling mother. They pulled a pop-up tent trailer, and as soon as the trailer was backed into the parking place, out jumped the kids with their fiddles. A couple of the boys removed a 4' x 8' piece of plywood that was tied down to the top of the trailer, while a brother and a sister laced up their stepdancing shoes. The show had begun before Dad had time to unhook the trailer from the van.

We chatted for a few minutes, and I asked him where he was from. He replied with a big grin, "We're from B.C."

"Holy jumpin', it's a long drive from British Columbia just to listen to some fiddle music," I commented.

"No, no," he laughed. "We're not from British Columbia. It only took us a little over an hour to drive up here this morning. We're from 'Inbacka' Cobden."

As I watched the kids perform, I asked him, "How many kids do you have?"

"We have five kids," was the proud answer.

"How many are boys and how many are girls?" I asked.

"We have three girls and three boys," he replied.

"That's six. I thought you said you had five kids," I questioned.

"Yeah, but one is a twin," he explained.

That story reminds me of another similar incident involving Heather's uncle, Kenny McHardy, who had a trucking business and owned and operated a service station on Highway 148 near the town of Calumet,

Quebec. One day, a family in a large sedan pulled in for gas. In the back seat was a set of two-year-old triplet girls, all lined up in their car seats like a set of dolls. As Kenny was filling up the gas tank, he peered into the back and remarked with astonishment to a bystander, "By Jeez, they're all twins."

Yes, indeed, Arnold Johnston is a patient man. Finally, after a tour around the world, I'm back with his story.

"Mr. Connelly," Arnold said, "I'd like you to know that farmers also have our own code when we get our tractors or trucks stuck. I've never had the misfortune of it happening to me, but a friend of mine told me about the horror that he once went through. This is how he described it . . ."

> Many years ago, I was cutting logs in my bush "inbacka" my place when I got my truck stuck in a mud hole. I jacked it up and blocked underneath the rear wheels, but couldn't budge it. There was nothing I could do but walk back to the barn and fetch the tractor to pull out the truck.
>
> I hooked the tractor onto the front of the truck and, believe it or not, I got the tractor stuck, too. Buried it right down to the rear axles. Splattered with mud from head to foot, I stood back to look at the situation. It was a holy old rippin' terror, that's what it was. By this time, my old hound was lying on the ground in disgust and embarrassment, covering his eyes with two front paws.
>
> It was in the fall of the year and it was supposed to turn colder that night, so I thought, maybe if I left the scene of the disaster, the mud hole might tighten up overnight and everything would be OK.
>
> I didn't say a word about the problem to my wife over supper. She could never keep a secret and would be calling up her friends on the party line before the cat had finished licking up his supper.
>
> I did the chores after supper and went to bed early so I could get a jump on the next day. But before getting into bed, I kneeled down on my knees and prayed like a son of a bitch that the good Lord would help me out in the morning.
>
> I was up well before dawn and walked back to the bush first thing. Well, I guess the Lord slept in that morning because, if anything, the truck and tractor had sunk deeper into the hole overnight.
>
> It was the longest walk of my life over to my neighbour's to ask him to bring his

tractor to pull me out. He pulled the tractor and truck out with only two yanks, and when he left, he said with an ear-to-ear smile that he was going to town to get his hair cut at the barber shop. "Hope there are a few old lads ahead of me in the shop. You know how interesting some of those yarns are," he added, fighting back a fit of laughter.

And that old bugger has been blackmailing me ever since that day.

While Arnold and I chatted further, I remarked how impressed I was with the names of some of the communities in Lanark County where he lived. My thoughts were that names like Brightside, Hopetown, and Flower Station strongly reflected a positive spirit that the early settlers had.

"Yes, Brent," he said (by this time Arnold and I were on a first-name basis), "others have also mentioned that. However, I guess I'm the exception to the rule, because I live on the top of Misery Mountain."

"It's never happened to me, but so many people get stuck coming up for a visit that our kids erected a sign on the gate at the bottom of the hill: 'The Johnston's on Misery Mountain.'"

Arnold Johnston on Misery Mountain, "Inbacka" Lanark, Ontario, "Where all visitors are greeted with smiles and hugs and offered a choice of tow chains for the trip home."

# Chapter 3: The Story of Shady Nook

*"I live in Sunshine, Ontario, sir, but I was born in Moonbeam."*

—Newly enlisted recruit responding to a question from his drill sergeant about his hometown

Lanark County doesn't hold all the rights to colourful place names. Northern Ontario is blessed with communities like Sunshine and Moonbeam, while Renfrew County, not to be outdone in sweetness, proudly boasts a place named Shady Nook.

The community consists of about two dozen homes filled with friendly people, clustered along Highway 41, a mile south of Pembroke. Neat backyard woodpiles stand next to fences surrounding adjacent farm fields. Huge, scattered white pines are a reminder that there was once a magnificent forest here. From the highway, overhead lights and brightly painted boards around an outdoor rink show that kids enjoy life in Shady Nook.

There are no streetlights or sidewalks, but occasionally an old hound can be seen trotting leisurely along the shoulder of the highway, checking out mailbox posts or calling on the frilly girl dog next door. At night, chances are a loaded log truck can be seen backed into a driveway ready for an early morning departure.

When we moved to Pembroke in 1975, I recall being intrigued by the name Shady Nook, which is proudly displayed on blue-and-white signs along the highway. Could anyone explain where the name came from? I would ask locals from time to time, but got conflicting answers, most of them far-fetched.

Then one day I learned the real answer. I was waiting my turn for a trim in Pembroke's Temple of Truth, Jack Court's Mary Street barber shop. A former shady mayor of Shady Nook was in the chair, so I asked him the question and this is what he told me. (Local historians should now be satisfied that, for the first time, there is an official and verified explanation of the origin of the name.)

Many years ago there were two lovers. The girl lived on Fraser Street in east-end Pembroke and the boy lived on a farm near Foresters Falls. Since they lived a fair distance apart and transportation wasn't always available, they couldn't visit each other as often as they liked.

Whenever he could, the young fellow hitched a ride into town, and the two lovers met in Pembroke's Pansy Patch Park. However, they found that there were usually people strolling through the park, making it difficult for them to visit privately. Next they tried meeting in Riverside Park and experienced the same problem. There was always somebody playing a fiddle in the park, so once again they were not able to enjoy their visits to their satisfaction.

Finally, it was decided that they needed to find their own private visiting spot. So, on a sunny Saturday morning, the girl packed a big lunch and they met at the Mary Street bridge, striking out, hand-in-hand, into the countryside to begin their search.

They walked and walked, and finally they found it—their own private visiting place. A nice little grassy knoll, shaded by the wide-reaching branches of several huge white pine trees. They spread out a blanket on the ground, had their lunch, and visited with each other late into the afternoon, until the cows in an adjacent field began the long trek back to the barn for milking time.

Against the background of a setting sun, the happy couple could be seen gleefully skipping back home, vowing to return the following weekend to visit some more.

It was on that day many years ago that the sweeping branches of the big pines whispered in the wind the name of that special little grassy knoll . . . Shady Nookey!

A friend of mine, Harvey Rutz, grew up in Shady Nook and continued to live there with his wife, Marilyn, as they raised their own family in the tiny community. He is a former logger, once owning and driving a log truck, and could often be seen in his driveway late into the night changing tires or doing minor repairs on the truck. I met him recently, and as we talked about his childhood in Shady Nook, he had the following story to tell.

Harvey's family lived in Shady Nook and attended a Lutheran church in Pembroke. It was shortly before Christmas on a bitterly cold night when Harvey was about ten years old and had the role of one of the Wisemen in the Sunday school's Christmas pageant. After the family had been loaded into the car and were pulling out for the trip into Pembroke, Harvey's dad discovered that he had no headlights on the old car. A fuse had burned out and he didn't have a replacement.

They were running a little late, so the pressure was on. After all, what kind of a nativity scene would it be if one of the Wisemen was a "no-show"? In desperation, his dad went back into the house and came out with a gas lantern. A plucky young Harvey was then perched on a sloping front fender of the 1931 Dodge sedan. One hand held the lantern, while the other was tight-fisted around the radiator cap.

That is how they arrived at the church—a Wiseman's journey with a difference. (It breaks me up to think of a modern-day drive down Pembroke's Mackay Street and meeting an old car with a young lad leading the way through the darkness holding a barnyard light.)

When I asked Harvey how he got home that night, he replied, "You know, I can't remember that. Maybe I spent the night sleeping in the manger beside Baby Jesus."

Talking about cold rides, in the early sixties, Herb Shaw and Sons of Pembroke operated a sawmill at Dusk Lake in Algonquin Park. They also had a utility pole yard a few miles down the CN track at Achray. In the winter when the bush roads were impassable, Johnnie Shaw, who managed the operation, would occasionally jump onto a slow-moving freight train and hang onto the ladder at the end of a box car for the short trip down to Achray.

Once again, it was an extremely cold day when he boarded a moving train at Stewart's Spur, as he had done many times before. He was always careful to do so out of the sight of the train's crew, as they would be quick to put an end to his hitchhiking.

But this trip was different. When the train approached Achray, it didn't slow down as it normally did. It rolled right through the yard, full steam ahead, and, of course, Johnnie was unable to jump off. With icicles forming on his chin and his arms tightly wrapped around the ladder, he continued the frosty ride for another three-quarters of an hour until the train slowed down at Alice, a few miles south of Pembroke. He tumbled off the train at Alice looking like he had just dropped in from the North Pole.

Harvey Rutz, Shady Nook, Ontario: "Our pine trees not only whisper, they grin a lot, too."

As Johnnie shared the story with me, he added, "Hrmmmm . . . it took me two years to thaw out from that trip. Ever since then, I left riding the rails to the goddamned hobos."

Before I leave Pembroke's Temple of Truth, I would like to share a couple of stories about its proprietor, Jack Court.

One day, Jack's wife, Marilyn, had some shopping to do at Pembroke's east-end mall. Jack dropped her off at the entrance and remained in the car waiting for her to finish. (Jack shops the same way I do—sitting out in the parking lot, listening to Ottawa's CFRA open-line host, Lowell Green, try to convince listeners to vote for the Liberal Party in the next election.)

Jack was parked next to a vacant handicapped-parking spot when, suddenly, a big shiny SUV pulled into the spot. Out jumped a strapping young linebacker who ran into the mall with Jack huffing and puffing right behind him.

Jack caught up to him in the food court and tapped him on the shoulder. With a puzzled look, the young hulk wheeled around to face Jack.

"Do you realize that you are parked in a handicapped place, chum?" Jack asked. "I guess your handicap must be mental." The SUV was moved immediately.

In two or three hours, Marilyn had finished her shopping. As they were driving through the mall parking lot on the way home, they were cut off by an attractive young blonde wearing a baseball hat, with a ponytail flying in the wind. She was driving a red sports car convertible and travelling much too fast. A collision was narrowly avoided as Jack swerved to miss her.

The young lady got out of her car and ran into the mall. Once again, Jack was on the run. It was his second trip to the food court that day and when he finally flagged her down, he asked, "Do you realize that is a parking lot out there, not the 401?"

"Are you a cop?" she asked.

"No, I'm not a cop—I'm a barber," he replied.

"Well, then, get the hell out of my way," she snarled. "I've got shopping to do."

The message at the end of all of this is that the next time you are having lunch in the food court in Pembroke's east-end mall and see Jack Court sprinting through a crowd of shoppers, stick around . . . something is going to happen.

And the next time you are driving through Shady Nook, take the time to walk quietly into a grove of big white pine trees. While you savour the fresh scent of a gentle breeze as it caresses your face, something very interesting may be whispered in your ear.

PART II

# ALGOMA AND LAKE SUPERIOR PARK

# Chapter 4: Algoma Bound

*"I logged on those damned side hills at Mile 100 for so many years that my left leg is three inches shorter than the right one. And that's why they call me 'Tilty.'"*

—Tommy "Tilty" Thompkins, Algoma logger

For ten years, from 1965 to 1975, I left the beauty of Algonquin Park behind to work and enjoy the splendour of Lake Superior Park and the Algoma Region, which includes the city of Sault Ste. Marie, Ontario, and extends northerly and westerly to communities such as Hornepayne and White River, and easterly to Chapleau and Elliot Lake. I was employed as a forester by Weyerhaeuser Canada Ltd, a subsidiary of Weyerhaeuser Company, a huge, multi-national U.S.-based forest products company headquartered in Tacoma, Washington. I was based at the company's mill complex in Sault Ste. Marie, which consisted of a hardwood veneer mill, flooring plant, and sawmill. In 1970, a transfer to the company's Mattawa operation returned me briefly to Algonquin Park, but more about that later.

Today, Weyerhaeuser Company is considered by some to be the largest forest products firm in the world. In 2006, it had annual sales of $22.6 billion and employed 49,900 people in eighteen countries. The company was founded in 1900 by a German emigrant, Frederick Weyerhaeuser, who made his mark by purchasing large tracts of private land on the U.S. west coast and building highly efficient sawmills. His far-ranging vision led to the company getting involved in the railroad business to transport important west coast forest products to the rapidly growing economy of the eastern states.

The company's success over the last century can, in large part, be attributed to the spirit of enterprise that obviously existed in the Weyerhaeuser family genes. Evidence of this goes back to the famous kidnapping in 1935 of nine-year-old George Weyerhaeuser, grandson of Frederick, who went on to become president and CEO of the company from 1966 to 1988.

Young George was kidnapped from his school and held captive for two weeks. A note was delivered to the boy's family and a ransom of $200,000 was paid to his captors. The case gained world-wide attention as reporters gathered around the family home in daily anticipation of a breakthrough. The drama ended one night when George appeared safely on his doorstep with a blanket wrapped around his shoulders. The world was relieved and the captors were subsequently apprehended.

The highlight of this story is that young George, recognizing the notoriety surrounding him, immediately put his own business plan into action. The day after his safe return, George and one of his friends pitched a tent in the front yard of his parents' home in Tacoma. His partner sat on a chair in front of the tent beside a table with a cash box. George was inside the tent, out of sight. Curious visitors were charged a dime to have a peek inside at the smiling face of a new young star.

To supply the Sault Ste. Marie mills, Weyerhaeuser had vast timber holdings on Crown land, and also owned several deeded townships along Highway 17, north and east of Sault Ste. Marie. The area extended north from the Soo to a few miles south of the famous little town of Wawa, known for its statue of a stately Canada goose standing guard over the town by the highway overlooking Michipicoten Harbour on Lake Superior. (I was always impressed by young Halloween tricksters who once painted large goose tracks walking down the highway and up onto the base of the statue. Only a stuffy old grouch could frown on such creativity, a feeling, I'm sure, not shared by highway workers who had the task of removing the paint tracks.) Weyerhaeuser also held timber licences as far east as Elliot Lake and was the primary licensee in Lake Superior Park.

Weyerhaeuser had two company-operated logging camps, one near Highway 17 at Mile 67 (Camp 67), north of Sault Ste. Marie; the other at Mile 100 (Camp 100) in Lake Superior Park. There were also several contractor camps and portable camps at various locations.

Logging was much more challenging there than it was in Algonquin Park. Rugged Canadian Shield topography and low quality timber put loggers to the test in delivering logs economically to the mills. Some of our logging

Weyerhaeuser's Mile 100 Camp in Lake Superior Park in the 1960s.

operations were conducted in the shadow of Batchawana Mountain which, at 653 metres above sea level, is the third highest mountain in Ontario. Logging roads were usually narrow winding side-cuts constructed along the face of steep slopes, and major grades were commonplace in gaining elevation to hilltops.

Most of the time, bulldozers had to have their blades angled to enable the construction of side-cuts. Dozer operators needed to be highly skilled with nerves of steel in manoeuvring these severe slopes and, from a distance, the dozers looked like little ants crawling up and down the hillsides.

Lake Superior Park, with an area of 1,600 square kilometres, is one-fifth the size of Algonquin. It is breathtaking, with its largely undiscovered rivers and lakes and mountainous landscape, which extends to the beaches and rocky shores of Lake Superior. Canoe-trippers face hard work to gain access into pristine interior lakes, but I have yet to meet one who would not return to enjoy the treasures that the park offers. It is by far one of Ontario's best-kept secrets.

The timber in Lake Superior Park was primarily yellow birch with minor volumes of maple, white birch, white pine and spruce, making it an attractive source of valuable veneer products. At that time, veneer logs justified the exceedingly high logging costs.

For the most part, the Algoma Region, and, more particularly, Lake Superior Park was virgin country. It hadn't been logged for hardwood sawlogs and veneer logs, except in readily accessible areas near public highways. In the early 1900s, limited volumes of softwood pulpwood was harvested along sections of the Algoma Central Railroad and transported to Sault Ste. Marie by rail, while the Agawa River was a primary route for driving white pine logs out to the shore of Lake Superior.

Over the years, timber cruisers employed by various forest industry companies conducted ground reconnaissance work throughout most of the area. Their purpose was to sample the forests to determine the volumes and values of the various species.

The results of these inventories, however, didn't provide much encouragement for the forest industry to undertake major investments in mill and logging infrastructure. In Lake Superior Park, the hardwood forest struggled to grow at the most northerly extremity of its natural range. Merchantable volumes were sparse and generally of poor quality, with the exception of the significant volumes of yellow birch, which yielded the high-end value veneer products. To add to all that, the topography was hostile.

John Dunfield is a well-known forester and author of two books on logging and one on the construction of log homes. He told me that, in the 1950s, he and Clarence Clouthier from Mattawa, Ontario, once spent two full weeks timber-cruising in Lake Superior Park on behalf of his employer, the Guelph Plywood Company, which operated a veneer mill and sawmill in Mattawa. His evaluation highlighted low volumes of poor quality timber and the presence of abnormally small veneer logs. Excessive road and other development costs added to the dismal prospects for profitable operations in the area. John's final report to his management ended with the recommendation, "Don't touch it with a ten-foot pole."

However, development did come in the 1940s and 1950s with the arrival of large hardwood manufacturing companies, such as Roddis Lumber Company, which was later purchased by Weyerhaeuser in Sault Ste. Marie, and Hay & Co., the forerunner of Weldwood in Searchmount.

It was a time when foresters and logging managers didn't have many of the vital tools of the trade that are taken for granted in today's world. There was little in the way of logging history to guide their planning for the future. No traditional yield volumes had been experienced or recorded, and there were no previous logging road systems to provide a framework for the planning of future haul routes. They had only crude topographic maps updated with rough field notes provided by timber cruisers and road locators. Modern electronic geographic information mapping systems (GIS) and global positioning systems (GPS) weren't on the radar screen, even as a far-fetched fantasy.

These early people were logging pilgrims, starting from scratch, and it was with a feeling of excitement that I joined their ranks, lacing up my boots and adjusting the magnetic declination on my compass. I was eager to conquer the frontier forests of Algoma from my very first day on the job. What a ride it turned out to be!

# Chapter 5: Blazing Logging Roads into the Wilderness

*"If those bosses with the shiny white hard hats want me to bulldoze a branch road into that friggin' godforsaken pile of rocks up behind Gargantua Lake, I shouldn't be starting from here."*

—Don Monto, Weyerhaeuser bulldozer operator

Beginning in the 1840s in eastern Canada, waterways were the loggers' highways. Small creeks running into larger rivers were dammed to hold back water so they could move logs cut during the fall and winter out to the mills during the spring rush. This was the golden age of logging in our country, and much has been written about the excitement and danger that faced hard-working and courageous river drivers.

Rivers continued to be used well beyond the turn of the twentieth century but, by the 1920s, they were starting to be replaced by more efficient truck and rail transportation. However, it took awhile before the river drives disappeared completely. For example, in 1956, as a sixteen-year-old boy, I worked on a drive on the Rouge River in western Quebec. That log drive ended officially in 1968.

In March of 1990, AFA logging contractor Ed Wunsch of Mattawa, Ontario, dumped his last load of pine logs into the Ottawa River at Mattawa to float down to the Consolidated Bathurst sawmill at Braeside, Ontario. For a couple of years after that, final sweep operations of the river continued to remove deadhead logs (partially submerged logs floating in the river with one end at or close to the water surface.)

Trucking operations began with the flimsy single-axle log trucks in the 1930s. The trucks were capable of hauling loads of 1.5 to 2.0 MBM (the equivalent of one thousand board feet of lumber), but were frequently stuck in mud-holes or were snapping drive shafts, transmissions, and rear differentials. (I was amused once by a skidder operator's description of a breakdown on his four-wheel drive skidder, which had both a front and rear differential: "I was pulling a hitch with four big hardwood trees cabled to my arse when I tried to get 'er over a little knoll. I guess I tramped 'er too hard and, bang! I busted my 'front' rear end all to hell.")

Next, in the 1950s, came Jack McRae's "goddamned tandems," which were able to haul up to 3.0 MBM, depending on the species. This was followed in the 1960s by the flat-bed tractor trailer units and tandem trucks pulling trailers. Load capacities increased to 5.0 and 6.0 MBM.

The adverse terrain of Algoma prompted Weyerhaeuser to introduce a whole new trucking concept into

Ontario, a configuration that was commonplace in the mountainous regions of the west coast. It was a piggy-back method, using big yellow-and-black Mack tandem trucks with the trademark bulldog hood ornament leading the way, pulling three-axle trailers out of the bush to the mill. After unloading, the truck drove under an A-frame winching structure in the mill yard. The empty trailer was then winched onto the tandem for the return trip to the loading site. With a simple back-and-forth manoeuvre under the loader, the frisky pup trailer bounced off the truck and was ready to be hooked up again to its poppa.

A major advantage of this system was that the weight of the trailer on the truck provided additional traction for the oftentimes uphill trip back to the bush for another load. The piggy-back method far outperformed straight flat-bed trailers, which usually had trouble climbing steep slopes or rounding sharp curves. This was always a major factor for those of us involved in laying out new logging roads. And that is where I started my time with Weyerhaeuser—hanging coloured ribbons on trees in advance of the mighty bulldozers, charting a course into the wilderness.

Carmen Hoffman, driver of Weyerhaeuser's "poppa and pup" log truck.

My first job was classified as "road engineer," and I took over from Paul Nenonen, who had been promoted to camp foreman at Mile 100. Paul, a slight, fair, soft-spoken man whose features spoke of his Finnish ancestry, was an expert bushman and could walk uphill all day without a puff or a grunt.

Friends and co-workers marvelled at how he could walk the side-hills of Algoma eight hours a day for five days a week and yet feel the need to attend weekend workout sessions at Vic Tanny's Fitness Centre in Sault Ste.

Marie. Wasting time in front of a TV was not on his agenda. Relaxation was a hot sauna followed by a roll in a snow bank.

Paul and I were members of the Copenhagen snuff-chewing brotherhood and would frequently come to each other's aid when the camp clerk had neglected to order in a fresh supply of the menacing drug for the van. (The van refers to a small inventory of staples that the clerk maintained for the loggers who were staying in the camp. It included a variety of items, such as toothpaste, chocolate bars, and cigarettes. The items were sold to the men through payroll deduction.)

Paul Nenonen, Mile 100 Camp Foreman - shouldn't be too alarmed at this little skiff of snow, after all, it's the tenth of July and winter's coming on.

I once stayed in a logging contractors' camp where the clerk took the forbidden step into the bootlegging business, and it wasn't long before he got his walking papers. (On another occasion, I worked on a log drive on the Baskatong Reservoir in northern Quebec when our French-speaking log-drive foreman fired one of the men. In a stern voice, he told him, *"Prens le pacsac et vois le commis."* Translated, this meant, "Get your packsack and go and see the clerk." In this case it was "Prens le pacsac et *au revoir* le commis.")

The work of the road engineer was to establish the ground location of logging roads to be constructed on all company operations and occasionally on contractor jobs. It was a fantastic job and gave me the opportunity to walk, snowshoe, drive, canoe and fly over much of the company's timber-licenced areas.

It wasn't long after my arrival that my new boss, woods manager Tony Vorlicek, called me at Camp 67 one night to tell me he would like to join me for a day or two while I put in roads in a newly developing area east of

A skidder operator setting chokers in Lake Superior Park.

Negick and Bow Lakes. I sensed that one of the things on the top of his to-do list was to find out if that young hot-shot forester from the Algonquin Park banana belt was any good and could he tough it in the ruggedness of Algoma. It was going to be one of those getting-to-know-the-other-fellow trips.

Tony left political oppression in his native Czechoslovakia and came to Canada in his early twenties. He rose through the ranks the hard way and began working as a chokerman on logging operations on Algoma Central Railroad lands in Algoma. (A chokerman attaches the winching cable to logs for pickup by skidders.) He later worked as a log scaler, logging foreman, logging superintendent and, eventually, woods manager for Weyerhaeuser at Sault Ste. Marie.

He was a handsome man who usually wore a shirt and tie when working in the office. However, when going to the bush, he looked like he had just stepped out of a Mark's Work Wearhouse poster in his cruisers vest, plaid shirt, and high-top Kodiak boots. His cheerful smile and good humour were signs of his enthusiasm for the job, which he easily combined with an eagerness to explore new and better methods of logging. He was very much a hands-on woods manager and was as comfortable and confident in a formal boardroom setting as he was walking in a pair of snowshoes during a blizzard on a side-hill in Lake Superior Park with a packsack on his back.

Tony was only ten years older than I was, and we became good friends quickly. The trip to Negick Lake was to be first of many as we often teamed up to explore the rugged, remote interior of Lake Superior Park. And, at the end of many of the days we worked together, there was usually an opportunity to wet a line in a good trout lake for an hour or two.

Within the next five years, logging crews at Mile 67 were scheduled to move into a new operating area several miles east of the camp near Negick and Bow Lakes. The area had not been logged before, and aerial photographs and a previous bush-plane flight indicated the need to construct a major causeway over a narrows between the two lakes in order to gain access into areas east of the lakes. The crews would be cutting there for several years, so we were facing a major road construction project. It was now time to put the boots on and go for a closer look.

We spent the morning walking through an area west of Negick Lake and had our lunch on its shore. It was a beautiful spring day as we looked out over the sparkling clear waters. There wasn't a sign of another human anywhere in sight and no evidence of any lakeshore cabins or trappers' shacks. The dense smoke from our small tea fire was the only relief from the swarms of attacking mosquitos, which we inhaled while eating our baloney sandwiches.

In the afternoon, we gingerly walked across a long and narrow beaver dam at the narrows and split up for the afternoon, each taking a separate route on opposite sides of the lakes. Tony walked north of the narrows and I was to check out the area to the south. (Recollection of that walk across the beaver dam takes me back to a previous day in Algonquin Park and another walk over a different beaver dam. My companions that day were "Hay Lake Joe" Lavalley, Eddie Coghlan, and a young Bob McRae. That story is just around the corner.)

Tony and I arranged to meet at the lunch spot at 4:00 p.m. to begin the trek back out to the truck, so we were probably pushing it a bit in our eagerness to walk over the next hill to see what was on the other side. After all, we were the first loggers to tramp that ground. Only the natives from Batchawana and Agawa had been there before us. There was a certain excitement to our mission and we didn't want to miss anything.

By late afternoon, we discovered, simultaneously, that we were both going to be overdue at the rendezvous point by nearly an hour. Since we had not travelled together in the bush before and barely knew each other, we were not sure what each one would do if the other was late. And we hadn't talked about that possibility.

We each shared the concern that the other might leave the rendezvous to go looking for his partner in fear that something may have happened, such as a fall or an animal encounter. This was compounded by the fact that there was a stiff wind over the lake which eliminated any hope of hearing each other by shouting. There was only one thing to do.

Instead of walking back to the narrows along the top of the hill where the walking was easier, we moved down to the shore's edge. Although walking was more difficult through the dense brush, it gave each of us a clear view of the open water and the shorelines of the lakes.

Suddenly, a mile or so up the shoreline on a point extending out into Negick Lake, I caught the flash of sunlight reflecting off a mirror. It had to be Tony trying to signal me. It couldn't be anybody else. We were the only two people within miles of the lake that day. I immediately responded by signalling him back. As we made our way back along the shoreline to the narrows, we flashed each other a couple more times. While walking back across the beaver dam together, we were a little sheepish about our tardiness, but the significant thing was that we had covered a lot of new country and were now sure where our main road had to go. Most importantly, though, I had passed my initiation, and so had Tony. It had been a good day for both of us.

There is a footnote here for moose hunters or others who find themselves travelling alone in remote areas: never leave a rendezvous point unless there is an extreme overdue situation, and always carry a compass equipped with a mirror or a separate mirror. (The old Silva compass that many bushmen use is equipped with a sighting cover with a mirror.)

Now a glance back to Algonquin Park for a moment and to the other beaver dam crossing mentioned earlier. I had just started my first job as a forester with McRae Lumber Co. at Rock Lake and was doing some timber cruising in the Louisa Lake area of the park. One of my helpers was an Algonquin, "Hay Lake Joe" Lavalley, who claimed to have been born in a canoe while crossing Hay Lake; the other was an old trapper, Eddie Coghlan, who had once fashioned a couple of beaver teeth to fit into his mouth to replace some missing ones of his own.

Our general manager, Donald McRae, had two sons, John and Bob, who later took over the operation of the company and still preside over its three mills in Whitney. As his father had done for him, Donald wisely set up a training program for his sons to expose them to as much of the lumber business as possible. Bob was an eager youngster of fifteen or sixteen when Donald sent him out timber cruising with us.

Although we really didn't need an extra body, his willingness to learn and pitch in quickly made him a well-liked member of our crew. His role was mainly limited to carrying the lunches and collecting wood for the lunch fire. But he did that cheerfully, while at the same time bombarding us with all kinds of questions, as you would expect from a keen young lad.

It was on a hot summer day shortly before lunch when we approached a huge beaver dam that had to be crossed. Upstream from the dam was a large flooded area with water depths at the dam's edge of five or six feet. We each cut a pole to help balance our walk across the narrow top of the dam. "Hay Lake Joe" was in the lead as he carefully chose his steps while probing the water with his pole. I was directly behind him with Bob following me. Eddie pulled up the rear.

All of a sudden, I heard Joe scream and saw him throw his stick into the water as he waved his arms and galloped the rest of the way across the dam.

"I stepped on a wasp nest. It's a monster son of a bitch. Watch yourself," he yelled as he stomped in and out of the water to the opposite shore while wasps rose like a cloud out of the dam. I was right behind Joe and may have overtaken him, I can't remember. Eddie retreated to the other shore.

But there was poor young Bob, standing about two feet from the threatening swarm of killer wasps. "What in hell do I do now? They don't teach this in the Bancroft high school," he thought to himself. So he did the only thing he could do, and he did it quickly. He dove into the black, grungy water of the beaver pond and swam like a trooper to shore with the wasps following in his wake. There, he crawled out on his hands and knees, spitting out minnows, swatting at wasps, and wiping black muck from his face.

In the meantime, Joe had collected an armful of firewood. "It won't be long before lunchtime, so we can make a tea fire here and dry you out, Bob," he offered with a smile.

"No, no, I don't want to hold you up," Bob protested. "I'm not wet at all," he insisted as he wrung a tea-pail-full of water from his shirt.

Locating roads was lonely at times as I usually travelled alone, a somewhat risky practice that would have today's health and safety experts reaching for their round-trip memo forms. But the solitude didn't seem to matter, as there was always new country to discover and new challenges to face in finding routes across the swamps and over the highlands of Algoma.

It was during this time, while I was walking alone for hours, that it became evident I had the world's worst singing voice. Bad enough to make squirrels run for cover and discourage the whisky-jacks (Canada jays) from joining me for lunch. (Reminds me of a time in Sault Ste. Marie when our son John came home from kindergarten with a note from his teacher saying, "John hasn't found his singing voice, yet." I signed the note and returned it with the notation, "Not to worry, Mrs. Dewar, his father is nearly thirty and has absolutely no hope of ever finding his.")

Sometimes I would be accompanied by a colleague, such as a camp or road construction foreman, who had a special interest in a particular area. At other times there were assorted tag-alongs that made it interesting.

In some instances, where the topography was severe and the bush dense, it would be useful to have an assistant to help flag the centre lines of the roads. On one such occasion, the personnel department in the Soo sent me a misfit of a summer university student. He was a lazy little bugger, and when I caught him one rainy morning turning cartwheels in the bunkhouse when he realized it was too wet to go to work, I offered him two "one-way" choices: he could either cartwheel his useless little ass down Highway 17 to visit his momma in the Soo; or arrangements could be made for him to catch a ride on a log truck. He chose the latter and that was the last I heard of him.

My next helper was a big improvement. An old cook at Mile 67 had a beautiful German shepherd dog staying with him at the camp. One morning as I was making my lunch in the cookery he suggested, "Why don't you take my dog into the bush with you for company? He gets a little bored sitting around here all day. The only time he perks up is when he sticks his head into the oven to catch a whiff of roast turkey."

I was a little reluctant at first, thinking that walking all day might be too much for him. So I packed him a huge "working dog's lunch," consisting of some pork hocks and butter tarts from the previous night's supper. However, he was in good shape and frolicked joyfully through the bush, chasing squirrels and barking at a couple of whisky-jacks that were following us. By lunchtime, we were close friends with his happy tail fanning the tea fire while he gobbled up his lunch.

The next morning at breakfast he greeted me excitedly at the cookery door and followed me to my truck when I was ready to go. By the end of the week, he was waiting for me near the truck. One day, when I was leaving the cookery after breakfast, I noticed him sitting in the passenger seat of the truck, just like old Freckles waiting for Hec. One of the men must have noticed him and opened the door so he could jump in. Some days he would take off out of my sight for an hour or so, but was always there when it came time to gather wood for the lunch fire.

His tendency to take off on his own brought us a little excitement near the Batchawana River one nice spring day. The dog was ahead of me, and I could hear him barking as I walked through a dense spruce thicket. Suddenly, I came face-to-face with a cow moose with the dog about twenty feet away, barking at her. We were in her calving area and she signalled with a couple of grunts that we were not to come closer. Slowly and with authority, the determined mother walked in our direction. Her head was lowered with eyes locked on the excited dog.

Luckily, the dog came to me when I whistled, and we retreated quickly. The next day, I left my disappointed sidekick in camp and went back to the same location. I could see from a distance that the moose and her calf had left the area. As a precaution, I took a wide detour around the site for the next couple of days.

My new friend was great company and came with me whenever possible during the time I worked out of the Mile 67 camp. The old cook was still his master, so as much as I would have liked to have him with me all the time, I left him behind when there was work to do in other locations. There was one exception, however, when I had to check out a problem in Lake Superior Park. It was an extremely hot day, and I finished up my work around four o'clock and returned to my truck which was parked at a roadside picnic site at Katherine Cove on the shore of Lake Superior.

It was a beautiful spot and too early to return to the camp, so I pulled up a picnic table near the beach and spread out my maps and aerial photos to prepare the route for the following day. I was wearing my hard hat and had taken my shirt off. Old Shep was cooling off and splashing happily nearby in the shallow water.

At one point I looked up and noticed a man watching me from the parking lot. He was driving a station wagon with Michigan plates, and had pulled in off the highway to treat his family to a swim. I waved at him, and he smiled while walking over to the picnic table for a chat.

I told him that I was a forester and was working on some maps. Shaking his head, he gasped, "You mean to tell me that you are actually getting paid for this? I can't believe it!" We had a nice visit. He told me that he was a machinist in a Detroit foundry and that he could only dream about having a job like mine. I reminded him that his dream would turn into a nightmare if he was driving on Highway 17 on a thirty-below day with a white-out sweeping in from Lake Superior.

Out came the movie camera, and he insisted on filming me working on the maps with his family huddled around the picnic table, watching, and the dog playing in the background. His two teenaged kids were very interested in what I was doing and asked several questions. It was a great opportunity for me to beat the drum for the forestry profession.

Every once in a while something with a different twist would come along. One time the company spearheaded and provided financial support to establish a family trailer park at Montreal River on a hill overlooking Lake Superior. It was part of an initiative to attract loggers who didn't want to leave their families to work in the bush and live in logging camps.

I was asked to locate a walking trail down a steep side-hill for the kids to walk to school. It was fun and took me back to the days when, as a kid, I had to walk to school every day, sometimes through blizzards, hurricanes, and sleet storms without the luxury of a school bus arriving at the front door to pick me up. (I have used that little white lie many times over the years to drive home a coming-up-the-hard-way point about my youth. Residents of Brownsburg, Quebec, would know that my family lived directly across the street from the school. Now the truth is out—I could be in my bed at ten-to-nine to hear the first bell and be in the classroom polishing up an apple for the teacher before the second bell rang.)

Ben Harvey was an old-time, hardrock logger with a determined, chiselled chin over which perched a pair of black horned-rimmed glasses. For several years he was Weyerhaeuser's representative at Elliot Lake, where he was responsible for a logging operation supplying a contract sawmill near the newly established community.

Ben and I teamed up one summer to locate some logging roads about twenty miles west of the town. It was a remote area without any previous road access, so the best way into it was by air. We hired a pontoon plane in Blind River and were dropped off early one morning on the shore of a beautiful interior lake.

The view from the air showed little development on the lake, with the exception of a couple of log cabins that may have been built by outfitters or trappers. A bright red canoe sat motionless in a bay as two eager fishermen cast their lines into the still water. The pilot told us that the lake spilled over with trophy lake trout and that the usual way into it was by plane, so that it hadn't been heavily fished.

"Whenever I'm passing over this lake and have an hour to spare, I set down and catch my supper from the pontoons," he explained.

We were in the middle of real wilderness, and there was a wonderful feeling of anticipation at the thoughts of exploring this new frontier. Arrangements were made for the pilot to return and pick us up at the same spot at 5:00 p.m. However, that was the best part of the day, because a bristling adventure was about to unfold.
The area had been burned over years before, so the timber was very scattered. In between the small patches of forested area, there were huge rolls of exposed bedrock where the fire had burned off the topsoil.

Within minutes, we realized that our compasses were not going to be of any use to us. Heavy mineral deposits caused the needles to spin wildly. It was also a cloudy day, so we did not have the benefit of the sun to guide us. Many times during the day we huddled over aerial photographs trying to figure out where we were but, since our photos were outdated, we had few ground reference points to work from.

Loggers and foresters have another code of the bush to add to the one about getting their trucks stuck: under no circumstances is one ever to admit to being lost in the bush. To do so brings some kind of a curse, so I have been told. When discovered to be lost by others and up against the wall for an explanation, the wiggle-out expression is as follows: it is not so important to know where you are, as it is to know where you have been. And, of course, everybody who has ever worked in the bush can always tell you where they have been and then some.

So, for much of the day we were close to being lost, but not quite. There is no need to explain the details other than to say that we didn't make a whole lot of progress laying out roads. The fact that we came across the same spot where we had our lunch in time for an afternoon smoke doesn't necessarily mean that we were lost. I like to think of it as time well invested in a comprehensive ground reconnaissance effort to gain a general overview of the area.

We made it out to the rendezvous spot about 5:30 p.m. To his credit, the pilot was waiting for us, relaxing on the beach munching on a fish sandwich.

"I forgot to tell you about your compasses this morning, but you guys looked like you knew what you were doing, so I didn't worry," he said confidently.

Since we were a little unsure of our exact route for some parts of the day, we asked the pilot to fly us back over the area, so we could pick off some landmarks. His was a small, two-seater bush plane used to ferry hunters, fishermen, and prospectors with their gear. Ben and the pilot were belted into the front seats, and I was sitting behind them in the cargo compartment on a rolled up tent—without a seat belt.

After takeoff, the pilot banked heavily to the passenger side. Ben and I were leaning over to our right to get a good downward view. Ben had his full weight against the flimsy passenger door, when suddenly it swung open, striking a wing support. There was only air between a startled Ben and the rippling surface of the lake several hundred feet below.

With only one ear holding up his dangling glasses, Ben yelled back at me, "Throw me a goddamned parachute." As the door swung wildly back and forth, I grabbed Ben by his shirt collar. The pilot, in turn, wrapped his arm around him and quickly banked to the left so we could reach the door to shut it. Since Ben was belted in, there was no chance that we would have lost him into the lake, but that certainly didn't occur to him at the moment.

It was a nifty piece of flying, and I am sure Ben's claw marks could be seen on the dash of that old clunker for a long time.

We stayed overnight in Blind River, and Ben didn't mellow out until after our third beer at supper. But that night we went to bed happy, knowing exactly where we had been during the day, and that's all that really mattered.

For obvious reasons, stories about loggers and foresters becoming lost in the bush, or any other place for that matter, are very rare. About as uncommon as pine cones on a spruce tree. (That is my opportunity to take a nick out of one of my sons-in-law, Reid Macdonald, who, when admiring a white spruce Christmas tree loaded with tiny spruce conelets, remarked, "Now that's my kind of a tree, one with lots of pine cones on it.")

However, there is one story I just have to share. Forester Bob Pick and I worked together for twenty-five years for the Algonquin Forestry Authority (AFA). He came to the AFA from his first job as a forester, in the Algoma Region, with the Weldwood Company at Searchmount.

Bob is considered by many in the forestry profession as a leading expert in the field of white and red pine forest management. But in spite of his outstanding professional credentials, Bob has one serious shortcoming for a forester. He doesn't know east from west.

Bob and I were scheduled to attend a meeting at the AFA's Huntsville office early one morning and had planned to arrive in town the evening before. We were travelling separately: I from North Bay; Bob from

Pembroke through the park. When in Huntsville overnight, I regularly stayed at the Sunset Motel, which was on the western outskirts of town, not far from the AFA office. On this occasion, Bob planned to stay at the same motel. We arranged to meet there at 6:00 p.m. and go for supper together at a downtown restaurant.

It was exactly 6:00 p.m. on a nice warm summer evening when I pulled up a lawn chair on the front step of the Sunset Motel waiting for Bob's truck to pull into the parking lot. I thought nothing of it when he hadn't arrived by 6:15. But by 6:30, I was getting a little concerned. Bob was never late, except when he was lost. Did we get our wires crossed with the overnight plans, or did his truck break down on Highway 60 in Algonquin Park and he couldn't contact me? Or, even more likely, was he stuck in a mud hole on some bush road somewhere? All kinds of possibilities raced through my mind.

As I thought more about our previous communication on the meeting place, it suddenly hit me. I knew exactly where he was. I jumped into my truck and drove back down the main street of Huntsville to the eastern edge of town. And there he was, with a peaceful look on his face, basking in the warm rays of the sun setting in the west. And where was he? Reclining comfortably in a lawn chair on the steps of another Huntsville motel—The Sunrise Motel.

"Where the hell have you been?" he growled. "I'm as hungry as a black bear in April with a severe case of lockjaw." Now that was believable. He probably hadn't eaten anything since devouring his usual mid-afternoon double-decker baloney sandwich.

Bob and I had a nice dinner together that evening, and as we climbed into our trucks in the parking lot to go our separate ways, I asked him, "Would you like me to drop by your motel in the morning and escort you into the office?" I didn't quite catch his mumbled reply.

What a man! Of course, he argues that it was me who confused the Sunset with the Sunrise motels. All I know is that the truth lies with the last one to tell the story. And for now, that's me.

There is an old expression that might fit here: "Sooner or later, each one of us will sit down to a banquet of consequences." I have a feeling that my time is coming as Bob Pick and his wife, Julie, make plans to set the table.

I have one more amusing story (amusing to me, that is) to share about Ben Harvey, one that happened several years after the aviation escapade. I had returned from Mattawa and was working as the logging superintendent for the Sault Ste. Marie operations; the Elliot Lake operation had terminated and Ben moved to the Soo as our road construction foreman.

Ben was a very meticulous man, as neat and orderly as a Tibetan monk. Everything had to be in its place, and he had little tolerance for sloppiness or shabby work. He had just picked up a brand new company four-wheel drive crew cab, boasting a glistening bright yellow body, which contrasted nicely against a black hood.

At that time, the colours of Weyerhaeuser's vehicles were similar to that of the Ontario Department of Highways (DOH). It was always a thrill to drive Highway 17 and approach a group of highway workers leaning on shovels and having a smoke. Our vehicles were frequently mistaken for those driven by DOH supervisors, so there was usually a scramble for the crew to get back to work. Of course, the fun part for Weyerhaeuser drivers was to lean on the horn and offer thumbs-up signs as they roared past the now busy workers. Gotcha!

The day after Ben had picked up his shiny new prize, I was driving with him into Duncan Township. It had rained the night before and there were a few mud puddles on the road. He tried his best to avoid splashing his new truck, but within minutes it was splattered with mud.

With a worried look on his face, Ben approached me. "Brent, I won't be going into the office for a few days. I wonder if you would do me a favour and arrange for a purchase order at the Esso station near the mill so that I can get my truck washed when I come in from the bush on Friday afternoons?"

At that moment we were driving beside a beautiful little stretch of water named Elizabeth Lake. A narrow road led down to a secluded beach. It was a popular swimming spot for residents of the nearby Garden River Indian Reserve.

"No problem, Ben," I said. "I'll make the arrangements, but in the meantime why don't you drive down onto the beach and throw a few pails of water onto your truck? That will do the trick for now."

"Good idea. I'll be working in here for a few days so that's what I'll do," replied Ben.

A few days later, I was driving by myself on the same road. As I passed Elizabeth Lake, I saw something out of the corner of my eye. I drove down to the beach to investigate. And there it was, Ben's brand new truck stuck in the lake about thirty feet from the shore. Two of the four doors were wide open and water was lapping at the floorboards. Scattered on the beach were Ben's hard hat, his lunch pail, and a chunk of chain. But no sign of Ben.

I continued up the road for a couple of miles, and as I turned a corner, I spotted him stomping up the road, his pant legs rolled up and soaked above the knees. Once again, his glasses were hanging from one ear. (This time it was the other ear.)

He was on his way to a gravel pit about five more miles up the road to fetch a loader to come back and pull the truck out of the lake. When I first saw him, I was so overcome with laughter that I had to stop my truck and huddle over the steering wheel for a minute until I recovered.

Ben heard me and walked back to my truck and blurted, “Connelly, you son of a bitch, if you breathe a word of this to anyone, I’ll throw you out of an airplane.”

And I didn’t tell anyone. At least not that day.

The loader operator was most likely the one responsible for telling everybody, because it didn’t take long for the word to get around. A few days later, one of the passing loggers erected a sign at the side of the road near the beach: “Ben Harvey’s Tow Through Truck Wash—No Charge For The Swim.”

After a couple of years laying out logging roads, I said farewell to Old Shep and was off to the Sault Ste. Marie office to the position of branch forester. However, whenever I returned to the Mile 67 camp for a visit, I was greeted by his wagging tail as he tried to jump into my truck for just one more outing and one more snack of baloney roasted on a stick over an open fire. There was always a sweet treat in the glove compartment for my old friend, a treat that he looked for each time.

The new job involved responsibility for the company’s forest management planning and silvicultural work, as well as supervision of contractor logging operations. It was a nice combination of office work and trips to the bush, and even the occasional chance to lay out more roads on special projects.

I had enjoyed the thrill of locating roads in virgin wilderness and then returning to watch bulldozers crafting a fresh road into the unknown, guided only by the flagging tapes that I had hung on the trees ahead of them. Then I would watch the arrival of crew buses, as cut-and-skid gangs began their harvest, to be followed by grasshopper-like boom loaders and the huge yellow-and-black Mack truck and trailers hauling the logs to town.

At the end of it all, the dreamer in me could always see a little piece of myself and my faithful old canine partner on each board that came out of the Soo sawmill. Can’t find job satisfaction much better than that, and what great stuff for management experts to postulate about!

# Chapter 6: Algoma's Side-Hill Gougers

*"At quitting time in the winter, we would turn over the seat cushions on our bulldozers in case it snowed overnight. On a minus-forty-degree morning, there was no snow to brush off the seat but, my God, that first sit was cold on the arse. By lunchtime, the old haemorrhoids would be stringing up lights and dancing a jig."*

—Emerson Grant, Algoma bulldozer operator

Within a few weeks or even a full season or two of completing the road-layout phase, along would come trucks pulling floats loaded with the heavy-duty stuff—three giant D7 bulldozers with blades angled and ready to take on the job of gouging out new logging roads on the side-hills of Algoma. The dozers were operated by Scotty Jamieson, Don Monto, and Emerson Grant, all three being experienced operators with big and sure hands to grip the steering clutch levers. They possessed a basic creativity in their ability to visualize what the finished road should look like.

The dozers usually worked together on the same section of road, or at least in the same general area. Sometimes a smaller D6 machine was added, depending on the conditions. Unlike today, where trees growing on the road right-of-ways are pre-cut by a cut-and-skid crew (includes a chainsaw operator and a skidder and operator), at that time, one bulldozer worked in advance of the others, bulldozing over trees and clearing boulders and other debris from the right-of-way. This was followed by dozers preparing the form for the road. It was common to see one machine several hundred feet away from the road on a steep slope scraping the soil of the shallow overburden and pushing it down to another dozer to be used to form the travel surface and to shape the ditch line. In the case of short-term winter roads, which were frozen to carry the heavy loads of logs, well-defined ditches weren't necessary, so the dozer blades were simply lowered to grade off a level road surface. In the modern-day construction of logging roads, excavators have largely replaced the conventional bulldozers, although where major side-cuts are required, bulldozers are still used.

How would a bulldozer operator describe working on the hilltops of Algoma? The best description I can think of comes from a logger I worked with at Mile 100, Duncan Jamieson.

Duncan and his brother Scotty Jamieson came to Algoma from Scotland, probably making them the only Scottish brother combo ever to fire up the pup motor of a bulldozer in Canada. (Bulldozers were once equipped with small gasoline auxiliary engines called pup motors, which were used to turn over and start the larger diesel engines that powered the dozers.)

After over thirty years of no contact with each other, Duncan and I met again recently and were discussing the challenge of road construction in Algoma. He summed it up this way in his thick Scottish accent: "Aye, Brent, me lad. When I was bulldozing on the top of those Algoma mountains, on a clear day I could see the sheep grazing on the hills back home in Scotland. On a soft, foggy day, I couldn't see the end of my cigarette."

The scene remains vivid for me: dozer operators bundled up on a cold winter morning, kneeling down on the tracks of their machines, struggling to start a pup motor. Sometimes a half-ton truck would be parked alongside to provide a boost for the stubborn little cuss. When the pup finally started and began its high-pitched scream, a strong arm would pull on a clutch lever with the other hand adjusting the throttle and choke. Then the big diesel engine would awaken from its overnight slumber with a snort and a puff or two of black smoke rolling out of its huge stack, followed by the loud rumble of powerful diesel pistons. A small fire made from a dry pine stump warmed the freezing hands of its master, as the big yellow monster sat patiently nearby, performing its warmup exercises.

The operator would then take his place on a seat, only partially protected from the cold by a canvas shroud which collected warm air blowing back from a reversed radiator fan. Then the long day would begin for the dozer, pushing, scraping, and forming a road through the wilderness. There would be little rest until it was time to shut down the dozer just before dark, when it would be fussed over by a weary operator, picking clean with a crowbar the day's build-up of mud and debris on the sprockets and tracks.

Glen Sundstrom, the company's road construction foreman when I worked out of the camps, had been a logger all his life and was close to retirement. He was well-known for his practical jokes and the use of hand and arm gestures when telling a story or explaining something. I have a couple of examples . . .

There are many disadvantages to logging in the winter; severe snow depths and menacing cold taking a toll on logging equipment are but two. On very cold mornings, it would sometimes take hours to start and warm up bulldozers and skidders. In many cases, a night man was assigned to travel around the job to start up the equipment and idle the engines for awhile to keep them warm. There were even times when bulldozers would be left idling all night. In later years, skidders were hooked up to portable propane heaters on cold nights.

Winter logging did, however, have at least one important advantage. The cold weather would freeze the roads so that they could carry the weight of the log trucks. This saved the enormous expense of locating, hauling, and spreading gravel during the warmer seasons. But there was a knack to freezing a winter road properly. It was usually done at night with one or more bulldozers, depending on the size of the operation, driving back and forth on the rough road with its blade lowered. This action helped drive the frost into the ground. The work was very monotonous. The operator's only break would be the occasional reflection of his headlights in the eyes of a curious timber wolf. Or the hoot from an owl in a roadside tree, protesting the intrusion into his neighbourhood. But that was about it.

(Talking about owls, one dark winter night, a Weyerhaeuser truck driver stopped his loaded truck where a bush road entered onto Highway 17. For safety reasons, drivers always stopped at that point to tighten the chains that secured their loads before proceeding down the highway. As the driver pulled on the tightening bar, called a bear trap, an owl swooped down and attacked him. He was wearing a heavy wool toque, but the owl's sharp talons still caused significant lacerations to his forehead. In my experience, this is the only incident of an owl attack that I am aware of.)

Scotty Jamieson was a high-strung Scot very much liked by all the men. He was very serious about his work, and his voice would rise a couple of octaves whenever he talked about things not going well on the job. He wasn't the kind of man one should walk up behind and surprise. It would be antlers in the treetops or face the risk of an unexpected backhander. Scotty worked for Glen Sundstrom, and Glen was quite aware of Scotty's reactionary tendencies.

One night, Scotty was out in the bush working alone, freezing roads. I was staying at the camp that night and some of us woke up around midnight to see Glen lacing up his boots and putting on a parka.

"It's the middle of the night, Glen," logging foreman Gordie Hoffman said. "Where in hell are you going?"

"Can't sleep. There was too damn much tabasco sauce in the stew tonight at supper," he mumbled. "I'm going to take a run out to see how Scotty is doing."

At breakfast the next morning Glen filled us in on his trip into the bush that night, at least the first part of it. Glen drove in on the road that Scotty was working on, and he could see the lights of the dozer in the distance ahead of him.

What a wonderful opportunity this was to have some fun with Scotty, he thought.

He turned the lights off on his pickup truck and drove for a short piece in the darkness, guided by the contrast between the white snowbanks and the fresh road. When he got close to the bulldozer, he stopped the truck and parked it around a corner out of sight. Ahead of him was poor old Scotty, all alone, trying to stay awake in the darkness of a numbing thirty-below night. In a near mesmerized state, his hands moved skilfully and automatically from one lever to the other as the dozer crawled slowly back and forth, over and over again.

Behind Scotty's seat was a protective screen which covered the back of the operator's canopy. A large winch was mounted on the dozer directly behind that screen. Glen ran after the dozer without Scotty noticing him. He took out his false teeth, tied a fur-trimmed parka hood tightly around his face and neck and, at an opportune time, jumped up onto the winch of the tractor. Then he gave Scotty a little poke on the back through the screen with a stick. Scotty wheeled around in shock to see an ugly, toothless, furry monster grinning at him against the background of the black night.

Neither Scotty nor Glen would elaborate on what happened next. Both are gone now, so I guess we will never hear the rest of the story. However, there are some things that we do know for sure: there were no injuries, no broken friendships, and somewhere in the Gargantua area of Lake Superior Park, there is a stretch of old logging road that is as crooked as a dog's hind leg and then some.

If Glen Sundstrom's hands were tied behind his back, he would be rendered speechless. Duncan Jamieson tells of a time when he met Glen on a bush road and they stopped to discuss a difficult side-cut which had to be constructed on a new section of road ahead.

"Glen got out of his truck," Duncan began, "and started waving his arms and pointing towards the hill, telling me how we should build the side-cut. Eventually, he returned to his truck and sat down on the front seat with the door still open. But he didn't let up for a minute, as he continued to rave on about that damn hill. Finally, as he was sitting there facing out the open door, he arched his arm and extended it up and away from himself to show me one more time. And as he did, he lost his balance and fell out of the friggin' truck, right onto his arse on the frozen ground.

"Aye, I wish Scotty had been there to see that. He would have pulled the bagpipes from out behind the seat of his truck and played 'The Road to the Isles.'"

Sometimes hunters are loggers, but most times loggers are hunters. And, amazingly, after over forty years, I have only experienced one conflict involving loggers and hunters. Hunters and loggers come from the same culture and there's an unspoken respect for each other. During hunting seasons, active logging operations are posted with "no hunting" signs to identify hunting-free buffer zones for the safety of the loggers working in the bush. However, what is more likely, the skidder and dozer operators are given some well-deserved time off and chainsaws are silenced for a week or two, as the whole camp empties and the men leave their jobs in the bush for the comradery of the hunt camp in another bush.

Back home, busy wives defrost and organize the freezer in anticipation of a delivery of fresh meat. A grubby husband will be home in a few days with his prize and a two-hour story about how everybody else in the camp shot at the moose and missed by a mile—except him.

Often young lads leave school for a few days to taste the culture, feel the magic, and learn vital hunting skills from their dads. The students may even get a glimpse of one of their teachers standing watch on the other side of a big swamp (or "moose pasture" as referred to by the old timers).

As AFA Pembroke's manager of operations, Danny Janke, once put it, "The hunting season is better than Christmas."

One fall in the Coldwater Creek area of Lake Superior Park, road construction operations were behind schedule. So much so that the bulldozer operators were unable to take time off for their own moose hunt. The bulldozers were having difficulty with some extreme topography and progress was slow. We were blitzing the construction in the area and had three bulldozers working there with the operators working out of the Mile 100 camp.

Occasionally, changes in the layout were needed when the machines uncovered large rolling ledges of bedrock and I would return to make adjustments in the alignment. I can recall one such time during the moose hunting season in the Coldwater area. (In those days, moose hunting was permitted in certain zones of Lake Superior Park.)

The area was well-posted with large "no hunting" signs tacked to roadside trees. The dozers were working close together in one location, but as I passed a branch road leading in another direction, I noticed tire tracks going up the road. I drove in to check and found two unfamiliar pickup trucks parked at the end of the road, one with an Ontario licence plate, the other from Michigan.

There was no one with the trucks, but it was obvious they were day hunters as they didn't have any overnight gear. I found it a little strange as American hunters in the park were usually accompanied by local outfitters. Since I knew who the outfitters were and didn't recognize the truck, the assumption was made that they were not local and perhaps were from the Soo, or farther away.

I left a note on one of the windshields, advising that this was a posted active logging area and that hunting was prohibited. (There were also several very visible signs posted along the road.) At first I gave them the benefit of the doubt, thinking that they may have parked their trucks in the no-hunting zone, but were planning on a long walk to hunt outside the zone. However, the prospects of carrying a moose carcass that distance sure didn't say much for their knowledge of the area and their hunting savvy. (Off-highway four-wheel vehicles were only a fantasy for hunters in those days.)

Since I wasn't a game warden and had my own work to do, I walked ahead of the bulldozers to check out a couple of trouble spots. I was standing on top of a big hill and could hear the rumble and the scraping of the dozers working on an opposite hill. All of a sudden, the sound of gunfire came from the valley in between the two hills. There were a least six shots, and after the shooting ceased, I shouted as loud as I could, but heard no response from the hunters.

I didn't feel comfortable with the situation and decided to walk back to the bulldozers to find out if the shooting had been close to them. Maybe I would come across the hunters on the way. But I didn't, not even a footprint, although I found some fresh moose tracks.

The first dozer I came to was Don Monto, a heavy-set and usually soft-spoken man. I had heard, but never experienced until that day, of Don's volatility, which was never very far below the surface.

Sparks were arcing off his earlobes as I approached. He had also heard the shots in spite of the roar of the engine. The hunters would have heard the dozers as well, and we guessed that they were within a half mile of both of us.

When I told him about the trucks I had found, the Mount St. Monto volcano went into a wild state of full eruption.

"Holy old galloping arseholes," he screamed. "I'll fix those stupid pricks. I'll run this big yellow puppy down to their trucks and crawl all over the bastards. They'll have to portage the goddamned nuts and bolts out of here in pack sacks."

"Now, hold on a minute, Don, there has to be another way," I pleaded. "I'll go out to my truck and radio into the clerk to see if he can locate the game warden at the park's Redrock headquarters."

We hadn't heard any more shots after the initial volley, so Don settled down a bit, but not entirely.

I radioed into the camp and stood by for a reply. As it turned out, the game warden was at the headquarters and his question was relayed to me: was there a dozer handy enough to go out and breach the road ahead of the parked trucks so that the hunters couldn't leave? He would pick up his partner and be down later on in the afternoon.

I told him that we could do that since the entrance to the branch road was only about a ten-minute move for Don's bulldozer. However, we wouldn't be able to restore the road until the end of the day, so the hunters would not be able to leave before dark. He didn't have a problem with that.

I didn't have to pass that opportunity by Don more than once.

"My pleasure," he said. "I'd dig a ditch down to China if I wasn't the one who would have to fill it in again." (Don and I had thought of felling a tree across the road to block their exit, but since I had spotted a chainsaw in the back of one of the trucks, we decided to walk the dozer out. These guys weren't going to make it back to camp for happy hour, if we had anything to do with it.)

The game warden was waiting for the hunters when they came out to their trucks. He told me later that, in addition to the unauthorized hunting charges and no moose to show for it, they also had a licencing infraction to round out their day.

"You won't have to worry about those boys coming back into this country—I lightened them up pretty good," he added with a smile.

And you can be sure that Don Monto held centre stage during storytelling time in the bunkhouse for the next few nights. "Yes, sir, I sure fixed those sons of bitches!"

I have had a lifetime admiration for bulldozer operators, beginning as a fuzzy-cheeked boy working for Canadian International Paper (CIP). For many years, the Caterpillar Company issued medallions to experienced operators. They hung on the end of a four-inch leather strap and clearly displayed the raised outline of a Caterpillar bulldozer. The medallions were the loggers' equivalent of the Order of Canada, and proud operators attached them to their belts for all to see, both on and off the job. It wouldn't be unusual at church on a Sunday morning to catch a glimpse of one peeking out from underneath a suit coat just below a vest-pocket watch chain.

The practice of distributing medallions may have discontinued long ago, I'm not sure. I haven't seen anybody with one in many years.

The first medallion, however, that I can recall ever seeing was in 1956 when I worked for CIP in Harrington. It was worn by John Fox, a seasoned bulldozer operator with the company. With that thought in mind, I wondered: Wouldn't it be nice if I could find a photograph of an old logger wearing one? It would be even better if I could locate a picture of John Fox, who has since passed away.

John Fox proudly wearing his Caterpillar medallion while receiving a plaque from Mansiel Wilson, - "Welcome to the Loggers Hall of Fame."

So, the search began with one of Heather's cousins, Joan Purcell, and her husband, Kenny, of L'Orignal, Ontario. They hit the jackpot upon contacting John's son and daughter-in-law. The family came up with a picture of John Fox taken in 1968 as he was being presented with an award by CIP woods manager, Mansiel Wilson. The award acknowledged John's role as the foreman on the Rouge River log drive, which was permanently terminated that year. Amazingly, the picture showed John proudly wearing his badge of honour as he accepted the award.

And for me, it was a step back in time.

# Chapter 7: Snow—How Deep Can It Go?

***"The snow in Algonquin Park may have been axle-deep to a ferris wheel, but up at Mile 100, there were days in February when it would bury the roller coaster, too."***

—Unknown Algoma logger

At first, I was shocked by the severe snow depths in the Algoma region, where accumulations commonly reached six feet or more in February and March. I can recall one year that it snowed almost daily during the month of January, and for at least six days that month, the Ontario Provincial Police closed Highway 17 to traffic between Sault Ste. Marie and Wawa.

On numerous occasions, logging foremen hired crews to shovel around the base of trees to provide an escape path so that cutters could safely fell the trees. Talk about making debt! Jack McRae would have thrown a radio into the next township at the prospects of having to hire a snow shoveller to help cut down a tree.

One day, as I was snowshoeing through an active logging operation near Baldheaded Creek, I could hear the muffled sound of a chainsaw ahead of me. As I glanced in the direction of the sound, a puff of blue smoke drifted out of a hole in the snow, like wood smoke from the chimney on a snow-covered roof. A falling yellow birch quickly followed, producing a huge cloud of white. I walked over to the fallen tree and was greeted by a smiling snowman climbing out of his frozen cave. While toting a chainsaw on his shoulder, he brushed snow from his face and reached for a pair of snow shoes.

"Sure beats fighting off those damned mosquitos and black flies in the spring," he assured me.

It had snowed so much one year that when we returned to work at Mile 100 from the Christmas break, D7 bulldozers could not open up the roads by driving directly down the road with their blades down. Instead, they had to push the snow sideways across the road.

After one road was opened, the crew arrived to start work and could barely make out the outline of their snow-covered skidders. The only thing clearly visible above the snowline was their portable maintenance trailer. It took them a couple of hours that day to dig everything out before they could start to work.

There was one positive aspect to the extreme snow depths. Previously inaccessible slopes were now accessible to skidders.

In non-winter months, skidders were frequently unable to manoeuvre on steep side-hills. It was just too dangerous, as the rugged terrain often caused skidders to upset on their side. There was an incident at Mile 100, when I worked there, where a skidder flipped end-over-end as it drove off a cliff top. Logging foreman, Brian Badelt, describes another occasion when a skidder pulling a hitch of tree lengths went over a steep rock outcrop, landing upright below the hill. "There were skidder tracks at the top of the hill and at the bottom," he said. "But no tracks on the way down." It was as if the skidder had become airborne, leaving its load scattered up against standing trees on the way down. Luckily, the operators in each case didn't receive serious injuries—they were only bruised and badly frightened.

The same slopes, however, could be logged during the winter as the deep snow served to hold the skidder back and keep it from running away or upsetting. This braking effect was an important consideration in operational planning.

To better appreciate the next story, it helps to know the layout of camp buildings at Mile 100. The cookery, bunkhouse, foremen shack, and office stood parallel to each other, with the front doors of each building facing towards Highway 17. An outside wooden walkway ran in front of each building so that the men could conveniently walk from one to another.

It was a typical day in January and had been snowing heavily for about twelve hours. I was staying in the foremen's quarters that night and it was still snowing when we went to bed about ten o'clock. There were six single bunks in one of the rooms, and Glen Sundstrom slept in the bunk closest to the front door. Log trucks were working a night shift, and the sand pit was located near the camp yard so the road maintenance crew, which was back and forth during the night, would plow snow from the camp yard. About three in the morning, we all awoke to a loud crunching sound.

The operator of a front-end loader was attempting to remove the snow from the walkway and zigged when he should have zagged, and the bucket came crashing through the front door. We all awoke in amazement to see a pile of snow lying about a foot from Glen's pillow. It took a little while to round up a chunk of plywood and some nails to make the necessary repairs. By the time the breakfast bell rang, the camp was buzzing with the story and old Glen was the centre of attraction.

People who live in Algoma take the extreme snow depths in their stride. They are hardy Canadians who don't get too excited about snow storms or would even think of calling in the army to bail them out. We lived in a bungalow in Sault Ste. Marie, and one winter I shovelled off the roof four times. The last time, I didn't use a ladder. All I needed to do was step off a snowbank directly onto the roof. I'd like to see somebody from Toronto cope with that.

Some AFA men taking a well deserved break from working in the rain near Kelly Lake in Algonquin Park. - L/W Ed Wales, Bob Coleman, Dane Brown, Bob Pick, Jeff Driscoll, Kevin Farr, Marty Laflamme.

# Chapter 8: Bunkhouse Blather

***"That hairy, long-eared hippie who came to the camp a few weeks ago stinks so bad that even the mice won't come into the bunkhouse anymore . . . I'm going to ask Ted Robinson to start up the steam jenny and hose that bastard down."***

—Jack Martin, choreboy, Mile 100 Camp, Lake Superior Park

The bunkhouse is the heart and soul of any logging camp. It is where stories are told, meetings are held, and friendships are formed. It's a place to relax on a bunk bed after a huge T-bone steak supper with a cigarette and a Mike Hammer novel. Poker and cribbage games are played every night on a big table in the middle of the one-room building, which becomes a home-away-from-home for forty or more loggers. For some, it is their only home for months on end.

It's a place to fart, and nobody cares. It is a place where yarns and tall tales flow freely, like moonshine from a rusty maple syrup can.

Johnnie Young tells about a road back home: "The government road running by my place is so bad you couldn't dodge the friggin' potholes if you were dead sober and riding a horse. There's one section near the old mine where it's so rough that the turkey vultures break their legs dragging off the roadkill."

Ernie Thomas describes a logging camp he worked in as a young lad: "The steak was so tough you couldn't stick a fork into the gravy.

"I mind an old lad back home who only had one arm," he adds. "He used to haul firewood from his woodshed into the house in a big wooden wheelbarrow that he made himself, and he never once dropped a stick. He could split and pile a cord of twisty-grained yellow birch firewood faster with that one arm than I could start my chainsaw and scratch my arse with two."

A French-Canadian logger working at Mile 100 was overheard telling the boys one night: "Back in the fifties, me and Gaston were cutting pine logs 'inbacka' of Bruce Armitage's place near Quyon, Quebec. The timber was so 'tick' that we had to carry barn lanterns in the bush to see where we were going. We worked one whole fall in an area no bigger than this bunkhouse."

If you are a people watcher, there is always somebody doing something a little different. Maybe it was repairing a snowshoe, trimming a beard, or slapping some Dubbin on a pair of boots to waterproof them.

One of my favourite shows was watching Duncan MacGregor roll a cigarette. I would stop whatever I was doing to take it in. I swear, an admission could be charged for a performance like that.

Duncan MacGregor and I worked together for McRae Lumber Co. at Rock Lake in Algonquin Park. He was the father of well-known author and media personality, Roy MacGregor, and was the subject of his book, *A Life In The Bush—Lessons From My Father*.

Duncan wouldn't give you an Ethiopian penny for a modern-day filter-tipped cigarette. No, sir, he had to make his own. That way every cigarette could be different.

Duncan loved conversation, and whenever he rolled his own in the presence of others, he just kept on talking, not paying the least bit of attention to the task at hand. He had done it so often it had become almost automatic.

First, out came a single Vogue paper from a little yellow packet stuck inside the outer cellophane on a package of Player's tobacco. The paper was then stuck to one corner of his lip, and as he talked, the paper flapped like a tiny white flag flying in the wind. Next, three fingers formed a claw, which extracted a small haystack of tobacco from the package, half of which spilled onto the floor, or if he was sitting down, onto the front of his plaid shirt.

Then began the rolling operation in the palm of his left hand as the flag continued to flutter while he talked. This next phase had to be watched very carefully to appreciate what really happened. In an instant, he removed the paper from his lip and placed it in his palm, giving it a half roll, and then at the speed of light, back to the lip for a quick lick. The end that was going into his mouth was crimped, but the other end was flared like a giant lily as tobacco continued to tumble out of the flower onto the floor. The last thing it looked like was a cigarette. It was just a funny-looking lumpy thing sticking out of Duncan's mouth.

Then came the finale, and I would sit there in anticipation, like a child waiting for the climax of a Canada Day fireworks display. Duncan would reach into a hip pocket and bring out a wooden match the size of a pencil. The match was lit with the flick of a black-and-yellow furrowed thumb nail, and the three-inch flame was touched to the open end of the cigarette. Whoosh! It seemed as if the whole room was on fire against the background of a smiling red face with a three- or four-day stubble hosting some scattered strands of tobacco. That is when we all ran for cover, as Duncan sat back in his chair to enjoy his smoke, talk some more, or maybe read a book.

Both the camps at Mile 67 and Mile 100 were within a quarter-mile of remote sections of Highway 17. Particularly isolated was Mile 100, which had no neighbours for thirty-five miles north to Wawa, and fifteen or twenty miles south towards the Soo. Both camps were frequent stopovers for stranded motorists or road-accident victims. There were also some unusual visitors and reasons for the visits. Occasionally, moose hunters would come into a camp wanting to hire someone with a skidder to pull a felled moose out of the bush. Or there would be a vehicle to be pulled out of the ditch, in which case, unless it was an emergency, a call would be made to the nearest towing service.

During the time I spent in the camps, OPP officers were frequent visitors, either to use the phone, request some help with an emergency, or check out a shifty logger.

One snowy night in mid-December, an OPP cruiser pulled into the yard at Mile 100. He was accompanied by a highway transport truck driver who had broken down near the camp. The truck was on its way to Thunder Bay with a trailer-load of Christmas liquor valued at many thousands of dollars. He was unable to continue with the load because the trailer had broken down. An empty replacement trailer was on its way, and the carrier needed a crew of four men to transfer the cargo from one trailer to the other.

The officer knew us well, as he often stopped into the cookery for a double-double and a fresh honey-glazed doughnut (some things never change). He suggested to the trucker that some of the loggers might help him out. It was close to bedtime, but it was agreed that they could approach the men to see if anyone was interested. Within seconds, fifty wide-awake and eager helpers reached for their boots and mackinaws, anxious to help out a trucker in distress.

A few minutes' delay was necessary to cut a deck of cards so as to whittle the numbers down to four. A couple of hours later, the transfer had been completed, and the crew returned to the bunkhouse with a few extra bucks in their pockets, ready for their beds. The police officer and truck driver came into the foremen's shack to thank us for the co-operation. The officer was asked if he was sure that all the cases had been transferred.

He replied with a wink and a smile, "I tallied every case, and there were only four bottles missing. I'm not sure, because I wasn't looking at the time, but I think they may have been dropped by mistake and were broken."

To be sure, camp foreman Paul Nenonen and his side-foremen made more than their usual number of visits into the bunkhouse during the evenings for the balance of the week, until the men left the camp for the weekend. (Each camp normally operated with twelve skidders, which were separated into three autonomous crews or "sides". The term "side" came east with the west coast-based Weyerhaeuser Company. Depending on the conditions, each side ran with three to five cutters to supply the four skidders. Each side was equipped with its own bulldozer, to build skid trails, and a loader with a two-man bucking crew, to process tree lengths into log products. A bush mechanic and a portable garage were also assigned to each side. Most equipment repairs were done in the bush with the exception of major overhauls, which were done in the garage at the camp. Presiding over all this action was a busy side-foreman.)

There is a footnote to the above story: Whenever I poke fun at a police officer, I'm struck by a tinge of guilt. I have the deepest respect for them and the work they do, and those I have known personally would shrug off the teasing with a smile and admit that they are fair game for the Tim Hortons thing. You can be sure I'm also fair game for them the next time I'm a few nicks above the speed limit.

I can recall an officer coming to Mile 67 to conduct a defensive driving course for some of the men. He told us of a serious highway accident that had happened late one night, not far down the road from the camp. A car had hit a rock cut at the bottom of the Mica Bay hill, and there were serious injuries. Two cruisers raced to the scene. A couple of transport trucks had stopped to assist, and an ambulance was summoned.

One officer went to the top of the hill to stop any oncoming traffic. Suddenly, a speeding car appeared at the top of the hill, and in spite of the flashing lights and the blocked highway at the bottom of the hill, it didn't show any sign of slowing down. The driver appeared to be mesmerized, completely unaware of the road ahead, and was heading on a collision course with the other vehicles.

The officer waved his arms and aimed the light of his large flashlight directly into the driver's face. But no response. Finally, in a desperate move to stop the car, he threw his flashlight at the windshield of the car as it sped passed him. The impact of the flashlight against the windshield jolted the driver out of his trance,

A busy log landing, Lake Superior Park.

enabling him to get his vehicle under control and stop it in time. The shaken driver got out of his car and stumbled around for awhile in a state of shock. The officer went on to explain that there was no alcohol or drugs involved; the reason appeared to be simple driver-fatigue, resulting from a direct drive from Thunder Bay without rest.

Why am I sharing this story when I'm here to talk about the loggers I have known? The image of that scene has never left me, and sometimes when I'm driving on a long trip at night, I'll remind myself of the incident. Maybe others will receive the same benefit of this true story told to a few loggers in a logging camp near the shores of Lake Superior many years ago by a nice cop.

There was another incident near the Mile 100 camp. A police officer came into the camp shortly after supper one night to report that a transport truck hauling hanging sides of beef had left the road while going down the steep hill at Montreal River. The truck had rolled several hundred feet down over a rock sidecut and, sadly, the driver had been killed. The cop came to tell the men that since the load of meat was impossible to salvage by conventional means, they could recover as much for themselves as they could pack up the hill on their backs.

That was all these old moose hunters needed to hear. Out came the hunting knives, chainsaws and flashlights, and several who lived between the camp and Sault Ste. Marie worked well into the night to haul out the meat and drive it home to their freezers. Yet not one missed breakfast at the camp the next morning. These were men who knew the true meaning of bringing home the bacon.

At the end of a day at Mile 100 camp, a logging crew returned to camp reporting that a single-engine aircraft had made an emergency landing on Highway 17, on a straight stretch near the Gargantua Road intersection. The plane was safely on the shoulder, and a police cruiser was at the scene with the pilot. In a few minutes, the officer arrived at the camp with the pilot, who asked to use the phone so that he could call a friend in Wawa to come pick him up.

The pilot was from Flint, Michigan, and was flying to visit friends in Wawa. He stayed at the camp for supper and chatted with us until his friend arrived. Before the police officer left, he gave the pilot a stern warning: "I'll be processing a full report, and there may be some serious consequences for you, so you had better not add to your problems by attempting a take-off from the Trans Canada Highway. You'll need to hire a float truck to haul that plane away. And I'll be up first thing in the morning to check."

Whatever the mechanical problem was, it could not have been very serious, because the next morning as we were walking to the cookery for breakfast, we heard the roar of a plane approaching. The plane circled over the camp a couple of times as our supper guest tipped his wings to us. No sign of a float truck—only a smiling pilot waving from an airplane. So much for the warning from the cop . . . can't catch me when I'm airborne!

On another winter night at Mile 100, a few of us we were chatting in the foreman's shack after supper, when a gentle knock was heard on the door. Logging foreman, Jean-Paul Beaudoin, opened the door and, upon seeing the visitors, groped for a nearby bunk bed to steady himself.

It was a mirage. Here we were, a hundred miles from civilization, when four very attractive young ladies dressed like ski bunnies appeared on the doorstep. They explained that they were working their way through university by selling magazine subscriptions. We were asked if it would be alright if they visited the men in the bunkhouse to attend to their reading needs. They were told to go ahead, but they would have to leave by 9:30 p.m., so that the men could go to bed.

Nights were long and lonely in a remote logging camp, so you can imagine the stir when these beauties stepped into the bunkhouse. A poker hand was left abandoned on a table, while Playboy magazines and Zane Grey novels were quickly returned to the little shelves on the walls above the bunk beds. Stinking socks hanging to dry over the stove were thrown under the bunks or into a nearby packsack. Out came the after-shave lotion and the chequebooks. Every logger in camp was a teenager that night, and the girls left with enough orders to buy a university.

One fellow reported at breakfast the next morning, "I figured it out this morning, I'll be receiving Chatelaine magazine for the next forty years, but it was worth it. It was the best night I ever had in a bush camp. The wife will be happy. I hope."

> *"Can't figure out kids these days. We have two daughters, one seventeen and the other eighteen. We bought them each a toboggan for Christmas and the damned things sat in the shed all winter—not used once, and we had over four feet of snow to boot. What the hell is the younger generation coming to anyway?"*
> —Art Chapman, mechanic and handyman, Mile 67 and Mile 100 Camps

Art Chapman was a large cheerful man in his fifties with a sharp wit and a perky smile who was always up-to-date with news from around the camps. He could offer an editorial essay on just about any subject known to man, and when Art mused, we all listened. (Marjorie Walker from Lachute, Quebec, and I were once talking about a mutual friend when she offered this comment about him: Ask him for the time and he'll tell you how to build a clock and what wall to hang it on. Well, Art may not have been in the same league as that guy, but it was close.)

Art was an all around handy man as well as the mechanic who repaired company-owned chainsaws in the evenings to be ready for the men in the morning. He travelled between the two camps, and always seemed to be in the right place at the right time. He had a shop in the garage of each camp, and whenever he was in camp, it became a meeting place at night where the men could catch up on the news while he worked. Many good stories had their start in "Art's Place."

One day in January, I was driving through the Mile 100 camp yard towards the garage when the clerk ran out of the office to flag me down. There was a telephone call from a member of the Sault Search and Rescue organization asking for our help.

But before I go on, a little about that medieval telephone. The call was received on an antique call box that was screw-nailed to a tentest wall in the office; it was the only phone in the camp. It had a crank, which had to be turned several times to reach the operator in Wawa. I can recall having to make an important call one day and cranked several times without any success. Finally, I lost my patience and cranked so hard that the phone was ripped off the wall, tumbling into a wastepaper can on the floor.

At that moment, the operator came on and, with sweetness in her voice, said, "Sorry about the delay, sir, can I help you?"

"Yes," I replied. "I have a hundred-year-old telephone in pieces in the wastepaper can and I need to make an important call. You sure can help me."

I can still hear her laughter.

Back to my story. The call for help came on behalf of a woman whose husband and two teenaged sons were on an overnight camping and ice-fishing trip in Lake Superior Park, four or five miles from the camp. The party was overdue, having been expected home the day before, and the woman, understandably, was very worried. The caller from "Sault Search and Rescue" sounded quite anxious about the missing group and explained that it would take him three hours to arrive on the scene with some searchers. He asked if we would have anybody available to go and look for them as soon as possible. I agreed to go, but needed to have someone with me in the event there was an injury, or worse. We didn't have a snowmachine at the camp at the time, so it had to be a snowshoe trip.

The only people in the camp that day were a female cook, a fragile cookee, a Scottish clerk recently arrived in Canada, and an old choreboy in his seventies, none of whom could have made the trip.

Then there was Art, who had not been on snowshoes for decades. But he was in pretty good shape, and so with some apology, I asked him if he would accompany me. He consented without hesitation.

We gathered up some first aid and other emergency supplies and off we went, prepared for the worst. I had been told what their planned destination was, and even though there had been some recent snowfall, we were able to follow their tracks from the previous two days. However, it was close to a two-hour trip and, by the time we arrived, Art was huffing and puffing like a mountain climber.

The man and his sons were out in the middle of the lake, fishing leisurely beside a cozy fire. We approached them and told them that we had been asked by their family to search for them. Surprisingly, the father seemed very nonchalant in explaining that since they were having such a good time, they decided to stay over for an extra day and had no way of contacting home.

I thought Art, who was a solid family man, was going to hit him over the head with a snowshoe. He didn't hold back on giving the man his views on the matter.

I have always been grateful to Art for his willingness to come with me that day, on what was a physically gruelling trip for him. You can be sure that the men who gathered in Art's Place that night received an earful about the events of the day, and about the roles and responsibilities of a father. It was on our snowshoe trip that day, when Art told me about his daughters and the redundant toboggans. Here's to you Art!

Ralph King was a tough, crusty, old log scaler who had been around logging operations for many years and was only a few years away from retirement when I knew him. His neatly trimmed crewcut and an ever-present White Owl cigar were his trademarks. I was told that at a company Christmas party, many years before, he announced to four log scalers who worked for him that they were being laid off. They would not have jobs after the holidays.

Ralph was not a procrastinator. He was strong-willed, opinionated, and some might say that, as an infant, he may have been baptised in lemon juice. But there was another side to this man.

An example of his softer side showed when he befriended a German officer who, as a prisoner of war during World War II, was incarcerated at an Abitibi logging camp near White River, Ontario. (Apparently only officers were held here.) Ralph worked in the camp and, during the war, supervised prisoners on pulpwood-cutting operations. The prisoner came from a wealthy background, and he and Ralph developed a close, life-long friendship. Ralph visited his estate in Germany on many occasions after the war.

Ralph was a frugal bachelor rumoured to have made lots of money on the stock market. He was a quiet man and led a simple life at his home in the Soo, when he wasn't living in logging camps.

I found him to be very stimulating and would often quiz him about his market savvy. He was happy to provide me with advice and reading material, and on a couple of occasions took me to his downtown stock broker's office to watch the ticker tape. I always appreciated his helpfulness, although it certainly didn't translate into any financial breakthroughs for me.

In logging camp cookeries, there is one rule not open to discussion. It is generally understood by loggers and strictly enforced by the cook or camp foreman, when necessary, that silence is expected at mealtime. Verbal communication is to be limited to "pass the gravy" and "where are the pork hocks?" I have heard two explanations for this. The first is, in the old days, prolonged round-table chatter sometimes elevated to the occasional fight in the cookery. The more plausible explanation, however, is that the cooks worked long days, usually rolling out of bed at 4:00 a.m. to start breakfast. Their day didn't end until clean-up after supper, and in some camps, there was a bedtime snack around nine o'clock. Naturally, cooks didn't want mealtime to become a drawn-out social time. Instead, it was expected that the loggers eat as quickly as possible and catch up on the news over a smoke in the bunkhouse afterwards. There would be no after-dinner drinks in these eateries.

Despite his quiet ways, Ralph did have the habit of talking out loud to himself—probably coming from many years as a bachelor, although I understand he did marry after I left the Soo. One night, we were having supper in the cookery at Mile 100 and I was sitting across the table from Ralph. The only sounds were the scraping of knives and forks on the plates and the occasional "pass the potatoes" request.

Suddenly, with his head lowered and shaking, Ralph growled out loud, "Goddamn it, what kind of a man am I anyway?" He probably had placed a "call" on a stock when it should have been a "put." I was tempted to answer him, but decided against it after getting a quick glimpse at the scowl on his face. It was a major feat to choke my rice pudding down that night without laughing.

Mile 100 loggers relaxing after supper and ignoring the cookery code of conduct of "eat up and hightail it."

Sonny Dugas was a company log-truck driver well-known for his practical jokes. From time to time he stayed overnight in the camp at Mile 67. The large, one-room bunkhouse was equipped with single bunks to sleep about forty to fifty men. This contrasted with the rather meagre allotment of four toilets, or "shitters" as they were called in loggers' lingo, situated at one end of the bunkhouse. Usually there was a mass stampede for the toilets after breakfast as patrons lined up, elbowing each other for position.

The toilets were equipped with batwing doors, providing a five-inch gap up from the floor. This allowed a logger to check for occupancy by glancing under the door for feet, with or without boots.

Truck drivers were up in the morning before anyone else and would have an early breakfast before heading to the bush to get the first load of logs of their long day. One morning, after he had finished his breakfast and while the rest of the crew were in the cookery having theirs, Sonny grabbed four pairs of boots and placed them aside each toilet so that they were visible underneath the door.

Sonny was half way to the Soo with his first load and laughing like a crazy man at the image of desperate loggers standing in front of the unoccupied toilets. Camp foreman Roy Perkins recalls that because of the disruption in the normal after-breakfast routine, the crew bus was late leaving for the bush. For his personal safety, Sonny slept in his own bed in Batchawana the following night.

Roy Perkins was the camp foreman at Mile 67. Tall and slender with the long-legged gait of a man in a hurry, he was always going someplace to check on something or to make an arrangement with one of his men. Like Don McRae and Johnnie Shaw, he frequently left the seat of his pickup truck before it had come to a complete stop. And his pickup was a crowd stopper—most times mudcaked, sometimes missing a tailgate, a forty-five-gallon drum with a hand pump standing straight up surrounded by a roll of skidder cable, and rear brake cables dragging in the mud.

Roy was always on the move, but never more so than at breakfast at Mile 67 one Monday morning. Roy had received word late on Sunday night that his old cook had been drunk since Friday night and was going to be AWOL Monday morning. There were forty-five men to be fed and absolutely no hope of finding a last-minute replacement. Where would you find a bush cook on a Sunday night? Nowhere.

Roy called upon his side-foreman, Jim King, for help. He fetched an apron from the closet and put on a chef's hat and a pair of black-and-white running shoes. The result: the men were treated to an outstanding breakfast, made their lunches and were ready to go the bush at the usual time. What was even more amazing was that Roy was able to find a good cook in time for supper that night. (Talking about practical jokes and now about camp cooks, Roy tells of a cook who once worked for him, who had a rubber wiener, which he would make sure was served to every rookie newcomer to the camp.)

Obviously, there was more to a camp foreman's job than presiding over problems in the cookery, but since an efficient logging operation depended so much on a well-run cookery, these problems had to be attended to. That reminds me of another incident that highlights what happens when things go wrong in the cookery . . .

A new logger showed up for work at the Mile 67 camp one day, and at breakfast the following morning was almost responsible for the camp's first cookery walkout. Even the cook was ready to fight. The unfortunate chap had only one eye, the other being a crude glass eye, which he may have won at a carnival or stolen from a pirate in a fight.

He also had a hygiene problem and appeared at breakfast that morning with foreign matter running down the side of one cheek. Upon seeing this, the men sitting across from him at the table started to gag and bolted for the door. It was left to foreman Roy Perkins to intervene with corrective action. Sure made for an unusual entry into poor old Roy's diary that night.

The availability of skilled loggers always posed a problem in the efficient operation of the two Weyerhaeuser camps. Adverse terrain, scattered timber, low productivity, and remote camp locations were factors in attracting and keeping workers. (One of the startling discoveries I made when returning to work in Algonquin Park after being in Algoma for a decade was that the logging costs in Algoma were more than double the cost of logs delivered to millyards from Algonquin Park. Much of this differential related to longer haul distances, but, for the most part, it was the abnormally low felling and skidding productivity.)

Therefore, camp foremen were always pleased when experienced loggers showed up for work. Such was the case when the Soo personnel department sent a new logger to report for work at Camp 67. He was an Englishman who claimed to have logged in the Black Forest of Germany and in the Rockies of British Columbia, felling the big stuff. Roy Perkins was thrilled. He had a new star in his camp.

On the new man's first day, Roy put him to work as a cutter. The fellow started the saw alright, but when he approached an eighteen-inch yellow birch, there wasn't even a hint of a directional notch (a V-shaped slice cut in the direction that the tree is expected to fall.) Instead, with one hand pushing on the tree and the other on the saw, he started to make a horizontal back cut before Roy jumped in to stop him. The star had not made a very good start.

"But I can run a skidder," he boasted to Roy. So Roy lined him up with a spare skidder and went with him to gather up a hitch of trees. Within minutes, the bloke had the skidder on its side. That was it. Roy's star worker had fizzled out and it wasn't even noon on his first day. To keep him out of harm's way before he could be shipped back to town that night, Roy put him to work making tea for the road crew. Surely that was something an Englishman could do without killing himself.

(Reminds me of another story told to me by Brian Badelt: One of the logging crews was using an old honey pail to make their tea. They would add water and tea leaves each day without taking the time to clean out the pail. One day, side-foreman Gordie Hoffman joined them for lunch. "Holy Jeez," Gordie gasped as he took a sip from his cup, "your damned tea tastes like hydraulic fluid." Gordie then took a little stick and proceeded to clean out the crud in the bottom of the tea pail. What did he discover? Some wilderness treasures—five little withered-up rabbit turds, one for each day of the work week.)

At the end of the day, Roy told the Englishman that he would have to send him back to town on a log truck. "I've tried you felling and skidding trees and you just haven't worked out for me," Roy explained.

"Blimey, but I need the work. I'm planning on a trip back home in a few months. Would you have a foreman's job available for me?" queried the cocky Cockney.

Then there was the story about a cutter from Mile 100, who unwittingly became the talk of the town in Sault Ste. Marie one spring weekend . . .

Some Algoma lads "doing lunch" while warming up the chainsaw gas, long before the days of WHMIS.

Solitary logger Mike Wells sitting on a pail toasting a sandwich.

In those days, there was no bridge spanning the St. Mary's River to connect Sault Ste. Marie, Ontario, to Sault Ste. Marie, Michigan. Travel was by ferry for most of the day, but it ceased running during late-night hours. When loggers came to town on a Saturday night, they would head for the bars in Soo, Ontario. Here, they would drink until last call, at which time they would pack up and head for Michigan, where the bars usually didn't close until the last customer had either left to go home, gone to visit one of the many brothels in town, or slumped to the floor to be scooped up and taken away in a paddy wagon.

The loggers would take the ferry when it was running. When it wasn't, they used a leaky old rowboat which was tied up behind the pulp mill on the Soo, Ontario, waterfront. In the winter, they walked across the ice.

Late one April Saturday night, however, old Ed from Mile 100 decided that he had enough and left his friends in a bar to walk across the ice by himself back to Canada. He didn't make it—at least not that night.

The next morning, a man who lived on the St. Mary's River about a mile downstream from Soo, Ontario, was on his way to church. As he opened the door of his car, he heard loud shouting from the direction of the river. He looked out to see a lonely figure waving like mad from an ice flow. It was Ed, heading out to the Atlantic Ocean.

Ed was successfully rescued, sobered up, thawed out, and back felling timber in Lake Superior Park on Monday morning.

And there we have it: another real-life example that there is always something to talk about after supper in a logging camp bunkhouse.

But, sadly, there is little in the way of bunkhouse blather anymore.

Thirty years later, the camps at Mile 67 and Mile 100 have long been closed down and all original structures removed. While some logging continues in the Mile 67 area by a new generation of loggers (more about that later), for the most part, loggers now commute to the bush from their homes. Few camps exist on modern logging operations.

The romantic era of logging camps in Algonquin Park is also long gone. When I first started to work for McRae Lumber Co. in Algonquin in 1962, there were as many as fifteen to twenty logging camps operating throughout the park. Today there are none, although logging continues at traditional levels. There are many reasons for this: the excessive cost of operating camps, the scarcity of good bush cooks, loggers wanting to be home at night with their families, and improved road systems and crew-transportation vehicles, to mention a few. Adding to that list are some of the wild shenanigans mentioned above. Operating a logging camp in today's world would not be for the meek.

# Chapter 9: Bush Mechanics, the Real Logging Heroes

*"An Algoma Steel foreman once told me that he knew things were going well when his millwright was on the job relaxing in a rocking chair. Well, sir, I told that son of a bitch, there'll be four moons in the shit pile the day a bush mechanic has a chance to sit in a rocking chair."*

—Rolly Goodfellow, bush mechanic, Mile 67 and Mile 100 Camps

As vital as a good cook is in the operation of a logging camp, equally as important, or maybe more so, was a good bush mechanic. Without one, the cook and his dog would be packing up for home and everything would come to a grinding halt. Open-heart surgery needs highly skilled surgeons; a logging operation goes nowhere without the knowledge and toughness of an experienced bush mechanic.

During the time I worked in Algoma, from 1965 to 1975, mechanics worked out of portable trailers located in the bush, near or on the log landings. They did minor and major repairs on skidders, loaders, and bulldozers directly on site, often in the harshest conditions imaginable. Only in the case of major repairs, such as motor and transmission overhauls, was equipment loaded onto floats and hauled into the garages at the camps. Here, they could be worked on under controlled conditions with ready access to compressors, welding, and hydraulic equipment.

In all other situations, the work was done out in the elements. I shudder at the memory of the many times I have seen mechanics lying on their backs on a thirty-below zero day, underneath a skidder, welding a hairline crack in a frame, or twisting on a wrench with frozen fingers. Equally as astonishing was the sight of a make-shift plastic shelter erected over a bulldozer, providing meagre protection from fierce winter winds coming in from Lake Superior, as a mechanic with grease from head to toe worked with numbed hands to change a final drive (a complex assembly of gears and shafts to drive the rear track sprockets).

The rugged Algoma topography often caused the failure of a bulldozer's drive-train components. Dozer tracks would also commonly become detached from the sprockets and idlers, rendering the machine immobile. Many times, these breakdowns would happen on severe slopes in the midst of a nest of boulders or in the middle of a wild swamp. If the machine couldn't be moved out to a road, repair work had to be done at the spot where the break occurred. Most times, the dozer would be able to hook its cable onto a sturdy nearby tree and, with the help of a mechanic and the operator prying with crowbars, the track would eventually be put back into place. However, there were circumstances when another bulldozer or skidder would have to be called upon to help winch the tracks back into place. It was dangerous and brutally dirty work, and if the weather was bad and the mosquitos starving, it was a living hell—light years away from a comfortable rocking chair in a steel plant, next to a watercooler and an air-conditioned lunch room.

Talking about dirty work, and as unrelated as it may be to the work of a bush mechanic, I can't miss the opportunity to pass on a wonderful story told by a friend of mine, Dennis Cooper, of Metcalfe, Ontario. But, I'll get back to Algoma in a moment.

One evening, Dennis's mother had to attend a meeting in town and left his father to care for their three young boys while she was away. Mr. Cooper was a well-known builder of barns throughout eastern Ontario, but was not as skilled in matters of a domestic nature. One of the young lads was still in diapers at the time and, in due course, had to be changed. Mr. Cooper put off the job as long as he could, hoping that his wife would return soon. However, the house soon became too small to ignore the situation any longer, so with much teeth grinding and gags choked back, he changed the diaper.

With the offensive item in hand, and fighting off a panic attack, he wondered,"What in hell do I do now?" In a desperate move, he raced to the front door, opened it, and threw the loaded bomb outside, where it was caught up in the branch of a frontyard tree. And that is where Mrs. Cooper found the family's new coat of arms, waving in the breeze, when she arrived home.

Back to Algoma.

Al Campbell was one of those hardy bush mechanics. Slender, wiry, and popular with his crew, he was a shy and soft-spoken man, when not prying the slipped track of a crippled bulldozer on the edge of a cliff in some godforsaken corner of Algoma. But when he was . . . all hell could break loose. Talk about a transformation! It was the mouse that roared and more. When Al was repairing a machine, his dark eyes flashed with the same intensity as Maurice Richard's when he streaked in from the blue line on a breakaway towards the goal. And when things didn't go well, his temper was an even match with the Rocket's.

One rainy day I was walking through a swamp at Mile 67 when I came across Al working with the operator of a D6 bulldozer. They were trying to winch a dozer's tracks back into place. It had come off in the mud up against a huge stone. It was a hot miserable day, and the black flies formed a dark cloud overhead. They were inches away from having the track back in its place on the sprocket, as Al put all his strength into reefing on the end of a crowbar. His face was red from the exertion. Suddenly, the bar slipped, shot back, and struck him just below the kneecap. The track fell off once again while Al grabbed his knee, howling in pain.

"That goddamned son of a whore of a yellow Caterpillar bastard," he screamed. He was so enraged that he rammed the crowbar about two feet into the mud and stomped off to kick a tree with his sore leg.

That was when I intervened and suggested, "Time to sit down for a smoke, lads." We sat down on a nearby stone ledge, put on some more fly dope, and chatted for a few minutes. Al had also heard Ralph King's diatribe at the supper table the night before, so we shared a good laugh over that.

Finally, Al stood up and said, "The worst part of this job is just looking at it. Let's git 'er done." He reached to retrieve his crowbar, but couldn't pull it out of the mud. We were now into round two as Al reached for his sledge hammer and started swinging at the bar to free it. That was my cue to depart.

I met Al at supper that night. He was all cleaned up and ready to dig into a well-deserved supper. "How did you make out with that bulldozer, Al?" I asked.

"I burned the son-of-a bitch," he replied with a little smile.

One very cold morning in March, I was driving my Jeep Wagoneer pickup truck on a main road at Mile 67, which had been opened the day before for the first time that winter. The snowbanks were eight feet high, and the road was only about a foot wider than the truck. It was like driving through a white tunnel. About six miles from camp, the engine started to sputter, before stopping altogether. I poured some gas-line antifreeze into the tank, waited for awhile and tried again, but it wouldn't start.

I walked back to the camp to get Al to help me. We drove out in his truck, then he began working on the carburettor with his bare fingers soaked in gas and freezing from the thirty-below cold. He worked patiently for a few minutes as I tried unsuccessfully to start the truck several times. Then the profanity started. I could tell that the dander factor was about to kick in and tried to brace myself for what was to happen next. He raised his arm in a threatening gesture, his hand clenching a cold wrench, and shouted, "I am going to kill your friggin' jeep—it's good for nothing but landfill."

It was time for another Ralph King story. It was obvious that we were not going to be able to start the truck, so we shovelled a turnaround, and Al hooked onto the back of my truck to pull me back to the camp. If he had planned on hauling me to a landfill, he sure was making good time, as he took me on one of the wildest rides of my life. As I tried to steer my runaway truck, going forty miles an hour backwards, it careened from one snowbank to another for six miles. I was exhausted by the time we reached camp, and it took a month to get rid of the kink in my neck.

Now to my favourite episode with Al Campbell, one that I had long forgotten about until recently, when I had the opportunity to talk about old times with Duncan Jamieson.

"Aye, Brent," Duncan began, "Al Campbell was a bonnie lad, wasn't he? And do you mind the time at Mile 100 when you tried to tell him how to start up a frozen generator?"

"Yes, Duncan, I still remember," I moaned. "I've been trying to forget for over thirty years."

It was a forty-below day in January, and all the equipment at Camp 100 was frozen up. Nothing was running, and Al Campbell was frantically struggling to start a mobile diesel generator to use in thawing out the logging equipment. It was not a good start to Al's day, and my arrival on the scene sure didn't help.

Innocently thinking that the generator was gasoline-powered and not diesel, I foolishly asked, "Did you check the distributor points and sparkplugs, Al?"

"Dammit all to hell, Brent, how could I be so stupid?" he replied quietly. "I'm sure happy you came along to remind me about doing that. I completely overlooked it. However, the blood pressure is normal, the kidneys are working well, and I'm expecting the results of a liver scan shortly. Now, if you can show me where the points and plugs are on this little puppy, we'll check them out. Should have her humming in no time."

You can be sure that my Newfie ears were ringing that night after supper when the bunkhouse chatter mill got underway.

As for the hard-working mechanics such as Al Campbell, Rolly Goodfellow, Ted Robinson, and the many others I have known over the years, there is little more I can say about them other than these men were not clean-shaven service technicians with impressive diplomas hanging on an office wall. They didn't wear freshly laundered lab coats and bow ties and work in modern air-conditioned service centres with piped-in stereo music. Not even close. They formed a special, hardy breed of mechanics that has largely vanished from today's world. They were in a class by themselves. They were bush mechanics.

# Chapter 10: Oh, Say, Can You See the Water Running Free?

*"A smile is a bright red bow wrapped around God's gift of life."*
—Brent Connelly, forester

Tony Vorlicek was my boss at Weyerhaeuser in Sault Ste. Marie for nine years, and whenever I think of him, I find myself smiling. It's not a hearty laugh or a chuckle. It's just a simple smile, reflecting a good feeling about the times we shared together at work. We both worked hard, determined to meet the challenges of the job head on, but there was always time for some fun along the way. We didn't socialize off the job. Tony had his family to enjoy; I had mine. However, what our relationship demonstrated was that dedication to work and having fun doing it can walk side by side on the same path.

In the 1960s, when Algonquin Park was under siege from an organized and determined environmental movement, a wave of anti-logging rhetoric had also begun sweeping across Algoma. Lake Superior Park, in particular, was targeted for an end to logging. In Algonquin, the conflict eventually led to the establishment of the Algonquin Forestry Authority in 1974 for the management of ongoing logging there.

A Weyerhaeuser production meeting: Cal Smith, Tony Vorlicek, and Bill Briffet.

However, logging in Lake Superior Park was much more vulnerable to termination than Algonquin. The licenced area was about one-fifth the size of Algonquin, and there were only two licensees in the park. Weyerhaeuser Canada Ltd. held the largest licence, while Weldwood, with mills in Searchmount, Ontario, had a minor area in a southern portion of the park.

Unlike the communities surrounding Algonquin Park, it was difficult to make the argument that terminating logging in Lake Superior would have a devastating impact on the economy of Sault Ste. Marie and region. Algoma Steel was the giant there and could, in the minds of many, readily absorb the economic shock of a few job losses in the Weyerhaeuser's Soo operation. So, although logging in Lake Superior only officially came to a permanent end through provincial legislation in 1992, because of the severe restrictions leading up to that time, the last tree was felled in the park in the late 1970s.

The 1970s were not good days for people in the logging business.

However, we at Weyerhaeuser were not going to go down without a fight. Bob Corbin, our branch manager at the time, had been parachuted in from the U.S. for a brief stopover. He was a huge man, resembling Zdeno Chara of National Hockey League fame, who took a hands-on role in fighting off the threat posed by environmentalists. He insisted that we all become vigorously engaged in public relations initiatives on behalf of the industry and the company. One of the projects that developed as a result of that renewed focus was the company's establishment of the Caysee Lake Campground.

A site was selected on the shore of a pretty little lake a few miles north of the Mile 67 camp, about three miles off Highway 17. A bulldozer was sent to build a road into the lake, and a logging crew cleared enough space to create a dozen beachfront campsites. The campground was complete with picnic tables, fire pits, and dry toilets, and was advertised on highway signs, which indicated that the campsites were free of charge to the general public and available on a first-come first-served basis.

The location had been chosen because it was in the general area of extensive silvicultural operations that had been undertaken to encourage the regeneration of yellow birch. Walking trails were established with interpretative signage to inform the public of the forest management objectives of these activities. It was a very impressive concept and well received, with much favourable feedback coming from the many visitors. During July and August, the sites were fully occupied most nights.

I was closely involved in setting up the campground by making arrangements for road and campsite construction, permits, and highway signage. A retired logger was hired to live in a trailer on site to maintain the campground and oversee usage during the summer.

However, we had one problem. We didn't have drinking water, and, without it, the only option was to have campers boil lake water. That wasn't good enough, so it was the quest for an underground source of good drinking water that led us to Lincoln Dunstone.

Lincoln was a tall, garrulous, suave American with a nifty David Niven moustache. He was a sophisticated tobacco-chewer and savoured an exotic imported chewing tobacco that looked like steel wool. He would turn his head slightly to the side as he loaded up, and not once did I ever see him spit. For a few years, Lincoln was the company's maintenance superintendent responsible for the maintenance of all rolling stock servicing the logging and millyard operations.

Lincoln claimed to possess water-divining skills and kindly offered to help us out. In keeping with the spirit of his offer, it was accepted, if not for anything else but to humour the old bugger.

I can remember asking at the time, "Tony, what in hell is this water-twitching blarney all about anyway?"

"I don't know, sounds like a bunch of hocus-pocus to me," he laughed.

A Google query identifies over a million-and-a-half sites where the terms water-witching or dowsing can be found. This amazing phenomenon has been around forever and never been explained satisfactorily, scientifically, or any other way.

The following is a brief explanation of the mystery in an excerpt taken from the Web site: http://en.wikipedia.org/wiki/Dowsing.

> Dowsing, sometimes called divining or water-witching, is a generic term for practices which proponents claim empower them to find water, metals, gem stones, and hidden objects over a piece of land or a map, usually through fluctuations of apparatus including a Y shaped twig, rods or pendulum. Some claim to need no apparatus at all, but simply to "feel" reactions.
>
> Dowsing has existed in various forms for thousands of years. The original use may have been for divination purposes—to divine the will of the gods, to foretell the future and divine guilt in trials. During the Middle Ages dowsing was associated with the Devil. In 1659, dowsing was declared Satanic by the Jesuit Gaspar Schott. In 1701, the inquisition stopped using the dowsing rods in trials. Dowsing as practised today probably originated in Germany during the 15th century, when it was used to find metals. The technique spread to England with German miners who came to work in the coal mines.

Skeptics of dowsing and many supporters of it believe dowsing apparatus has no special powers but simply amplifies small but otherwise imperceptible movements of the hands, which has long been established to be the ideomotor effect. Most investigators believe the small movements arise from the expectations of the dowser. Supporters say the dowser has a subliminal sensitivity to the environment, perhaps via electroception, magnetoception, or telluric currents.

Some say dowsing is better classified as a paranormal belief than as a pseudoscience. In pseudoscience, scientific sounding jargon is used and explanations are unable to be supported scientifically. Dowsers, however, cannot explain the source of their powers apart from magnetic fields and auras, and simply "believe" they can dowse, making it more a matter of faith than science.

Oh, what a treat it would have been to have been able to throw some of that pseudoscience stuff out for open discussion over a game of crib in the bunkhouse at Mile 67 on a rainy night.

One day, Tony and I were travelling to Mile 100 and asked Lincoln to come with us to see if he could work his magic in finding water at the campground. We tried to hide our skepticism when we picked him up at the maintenance centre. He was carrying a small attaché case and smiling confidently that, before the day ended, we would be sipping cool, clear water from a newly discovered geyser.

Lincoln proudly opened up the case to display its contents. There, lying in a bed of red velvet cloth, were the tools of his trade: two shiny, L-shaped brass rods.

As we walked to the truck with old Lincoln gripping tightly onto the handle of his attaché case, I whispered to Tony, "He looks like one of Al Capone's men with a machine gun on his way to Luigi's restaurant to pull off a mob wipeout."

We arrived at the campground, which was still under construction, and decided to start the search a hundred feet away from the lake. Before Lincoln began, however, he demonstrated the procedure to us. He explained that the rods had to be held tightly about six inches apart, close to, and high up on the chest. The long ends of the "L" faced straight ahead and at right angles to his body. He showed us how to hold the short ends of the "L" with an overhand grip and then a twist of the hands against the chest so that some tension would be created in the grip. It wasn't just a simple matter of grabbing the rods any which way. No, sir, we're talking magnetoception and subliminal sensitivity here.

By this time, we had been joined by a backhoe operator and a truck driver who were working close by and were curious about this voodoo ritual. Before he started, Lincoln insisted that each one of us try our hands at dowsing. He told us that for most people there would be no reaction when walking over a vein of water. But, who knew, there could be a star amongst this motley group of disbelievers.

He had each one of us cut a small, forked maple branch about three feet long with eight-inch forks. He showed us how to hold the branches and explained that if we had the power and walked over a vein, there would be a strong pull of the tip of the stick towards the ground.

So off we went, with Lincoln in the lead, as he walked slowly and silently through the bush. Directly behind him were the two loggers, followed by me and Tony at the end of the line. We walked back and forth for about twenty minutes with no results. Suddenly, we heard a soft gasp from Lincoln and could see that his rods had crossed. We stopped and he backed up about four feet, changed his direction by six feet to his left, and continued to walk ahead. He stopped once more when his rods crossed for the second time. He repeated the same pattern, this time offsetting another six feet and, once again, another hit.

"We've found the mother lode, lads. Another Old Faithful right here in the middle of the Algoma Highlands. Now it's your turn to try," he shouted excitedly.

The loggers followed his path, walking back and forth without any movement of their branches. I was next, and when I came close to the spot where Lincoln's rods had first crossed, I could feel a slight tug on my branch. And then, bang! It was like a big trout on the end of a fly rod as the rod dived to the ground. The pull was so strong that I couldn't keep the stick from dipping, and when I gripped the forks harder, there was slight discomfort on the inside of my palms.

Wow! I had the magic, too. So much for the theory about faith. Until that moment, I had no faith whatsoever in what I had always believed was some sort of bizarre craft performed by witches—and now I was one of them. It was a most unbelievable and strange sensation, as I realized I had now been given a peek into the world of the supernatural.

Maybe now I could start Al Campbell's generator by chanting "abracadabra" and waving my dowsing rod over it? Wouldn't that give him something to chew on in the bunkhouse?

It was Tony's turn next, and what a sight that turned out to be.

When he approached the spot where Lincoln and I had our out-of-world experience, I could see a weird look come over his face as he struggled to control his stick. Then, whack! Instead of dipping to the ground, the stick snapped back and smacked poor old Tony right between the eyes.

Tony's protons must have got mixed up with his neutrons, and what a laugh we all had over his screwed-up electro-magnetic field. I told him it was because he was Catholic and Lincoln and I were Protestants. Lincoln mapped out the location of the vein, while explaining that underground water in that part of the country ran from west to east. He also said that some people claim they are able to estimate the depth of the vein by the strength of the pull. His experience with dowsing didn't support that, although he didn't discount it either. Lincoln chose a spot as close as possible to the lake and the backhoe found a beautiful pool of water after digging for only fifteen minutes—mission accomplished. We had found water, and the world of dowsing had gained two more practitioners, one negative and one positive.

Over the years I have read a lot on the subject, but have no more understanding of the strange empowerment now than I did then. I have only dowsed for water on a few occasions since that day at Caysee Lake and remain puzzled about three things: dowsing doesn't work over open water, like a lake or creek; I was a hard-core skeptic and it worked for me; and in my experience there is no reaction if the water is flowing through pipes, only if it is in a natural undisturbed underground vein. Perplexing, for sure.

The following is an account of an opportunity I once had to demonstrate my newly found dowsing skills. It occurred several years after my dramatic coming-out at Caysee Lake.

Logging contractor Walter Dombroski was building a new logging camp in the Basin Depot area of Algonquin Park. The layout of the camp was such that the cookery and bunkhouse were located along the western edge of the area cleared for the camp. This was to enable the loaded log trucks to enter the camp yard from the main road and return to the road without having to back up.

Walter brought in his backhoe and began digging close to the cookery. He was hoping to find a source of water as close as possible to the camp buildings, but came up with a blank. I offered to dowse to see what that would turn up. I started at the cookery and slowly made my way across the yard without any success. The farther away I got from the cookery, the bigger the frown on Walter's face grew.

"Goddamn it, Brent," he said, "find me some water near my cookery. I don't want to have to dig a ditch into the next township. You're not paying enough for me to afford that bullshit. All I have so far this year from your friggin' logging job is a sore back and a packsack filled with cheque stubs, and the only thing I went home with from last year's job was a leaky pail full of rusty pennies. Damn it all to hell!"

"I can find water if it's here, Walter, but I can't manufacture it," I snapped back at him.

Finally, at the far edge of the yard about two hundred feet from the cookery, I hit the jackpot. "There you are, Walter," I said as I climbed into my truck to leave. "You'll find water there. Now you can fire up your backhoe and dig that ditch."

But that stubborn old bugger didn't dig the ditch, at least not that day anyway. He wanted a second opinion. The following day, Walter had a visitor to his camp, Joe Lorbetskie, a scaling supervisor for the Ministry of Natural Resources. Joe also had the magic.

"Can you find me some water, Joe?" Walter asked as he pointed to the bush line at the opposite end of the yard where I had placed a stake, "That son of a bitch of a Brent Connelly told me that's the only place there's water, and it's a mile away from my cookery."

Joe told me later that he dowsed the whole yard and didn't feel a tug on his stick until he approached the stake. To this day, whenever we meet each other, Walter and I have a good laugh over his bull-headed ways—at least I do.

Now back to the Caysee Lake campground for one final story; a story that can now safely be told in light of a sufficient separation in time and place from the day the incident occurred—over 35 years later and 560 miles away. That should be safe enough. I think.

The Caysee Lake campground operated successfully for several years. Each year, prior to its opening in mid-June, a couple of loggers from the camp at Mile 67 were dispatched to clean up the campground and the road leading into it. There would be the usual over-winter accumulation of downed trees and woody debris.

It was a beautiful warm sunny afternoon in early May, and I was travelling to Mile 100 to spend the night at the camp. I was driving a company-owned Volkswagen Beetle, and when approaching the campground entrance, I decided to take a quick drive into the campground to see what clean-up work had to be done and if Lincoln's geyser had remained faithful over the winter. I had enough time for a drive-through inspection and be up to the camp in time for supper.

The road into the campground was a branch road leading from another logging road. It was a narrow one-way loop that entered the campground from the east and exited to the west, back out to the logging road. Large yellow birch and maple trees loomed close to the travel surface, with their massive tops intertwined. After spring leaf-out, the road was like a beautiful green tunnel with a glimpse of open blue water at the other end. It was magical.

We had deliberately kept the right-of-way narrow so that it would be best suited to travellers with tents and small trailers. There was concern that a large hill on the logging road would be a problem for larger motorhomes and trailers.

I was zipping along at a pretty fair clip and had not expected to meet anybody else in the campground at such an early date. There were still numerous patches of snow on the ground and the Canada geese had just set their compass for their northerly flight towards Wawa. There wasn't a black fly or mosquito in sight. It was an absolutely gorgeous Algoma day.

I could see the lake in the distance, and when I came to the first campsite, I was flabbergasted at the sight of a small red car parked down near the beach where there were two picnic tables pulled up beside each other. On top of the tables, two-bikini clad young ladies sunbathed in the warm sun, enjoying their own little private paradise. By all that's holy, was this the logger's mirage they used to talk about at evening storytelling time in the bunkhouse?

Suddenly, while I rubber-necked to see if there were any downed trees near the girls' campsite, I caught a glimpse of a black figure out of the corner of my eye. A large bull moose charged out of the bush from the other side of the road, directly into the path of my quickly moving vehicle. Instantly, I swerved to the left to miss the moose and ran up on a slope which came down to the side of the road. Bang! Head on into a 150-year-old yellow birch tree.

I sheepishly got out of the car to inspect the damage and found the flimsy front bumper pushed right back into the hood of the car. The girls had heard the sound of impact and ran over to check on me. After they discovered I wasn't injured, they weren't shy to show their amusement over the situation and my obvious embarrassment. It seemed they thought that they were the cause of my distraction and subsequent mishap. They hadn't seen the moose and looked puzzled when I explained it was the stupid animal that startled me and not them.

We chatted as I hooked a chain onto the tree to straighten my bumper. They explained that they were university students driving to Banff for summer employment, had seen the highway signs and decided to camp overnight at Caysee Lake. The girls would certainly have an unusual diary entry for that day. As for me, I didn't go near my diary for the balance of the week.

True story? No question! All except the moose part. That was a fabrication, bordering on a lie. And it was the same fabrication that I used when completing my internal company accident report. So, for those who may have remembered hearing about my experience at Caysee Lake on that beautiful spring day, well, now you know the rest of the story.

At the end of it all, somewhere near a lovely little lake, deep in the highlands of Algoma, the water is running free. It's running there for you. It's running there for me.

# Chapter 11: A Little Bit of Heaven on Stilts

*"I don't have a payload on board if I can lift 'er off the pond and clear the tree line on the first try."*

—Unknown Algoma bush pilot

One of the most ambitious main-haul road projects that I was involved in during my time with Weyerhaeuser was the O'Connor Road in Lake Superior Park. Highway 17 bisected the park in a north-south direction, at some points coming close to Lake Superior, while the Algoma Central Railway traced the eastern boundary of the park, parallel to the highway. In between the two was a vast area of previously inaccessible timber which had never been cut before. The O'Connor Road would connect the highway to the railway near the former O'Connor Siding, a distance of twenty miles, depending on the route selected. (No logging road in Lake Superior Park ever ran in a straight line.)

There had been previous flights over the general route and several options were outlined on aerial photographs and maps. The rugged topography was adverse with its massive areas of vertical rock outcroppings. The extensive waterways, in most cases, ran opposite to the desired east-west alignment of the road. There were numerous lakes and streams alive with trout, and large swamps blocked us at almost every turn.

It was vital that an extensive step-by-step ground examination be carried out in the selection of the best right-of-way. Tony Vorlicek and I teamed up to make several trips on behalf of the project, four of which stand out clearly in my memory, the last being one of the most remarkable overnight stays in the bush I have ever experienced. One that would make the keenest outdoorsperson pant with excitement.

The duration of the outings ranged from two- or three-day trips to week-long excursions. Travel was by air, canoe, and on foot, many times wearing snowshoes. Access by truck was usually limited to a couple of miles from public roads. In those days, ATVs and snow machines were still in the introductory stage. Initial access into some remote areas was by train, which we boarded in Sault Ste. Marie with our gear and canoe.

The first aerial trip we took together was on a jalopy we rented from a local outfitter. I recall early one morning when we took off from Wawa Lake in the antique single-engine plane. My fear at the sight of the plane may have something to do with my inability to recall a detailed description of it, except that it was very scary-looking. It was a foggy morning, but the grizzly old pilot explained to us, as he choked back a heavy smoker's cough, that as long as he could see the prop spinning in front of him, we were good to go.

A large Campbell diesel generator, which looked like it weighed two tons, occupied the plane's cargo section. We were told that, after we were dropped off at our destination on an interior lake, the generator was being flown into a gold mining camp east of Hawk Junction.

The pilot sat in the plane's only seat, while Tony and I squatted nervously in the back on two five-gallon cans filled with gasoline.

This trip occurred after my flight with Ben Harvey, so I was pleased to be sitting in the rear of the plane and not beside a see-through front door.

As soon as we were settled in, the pilot took out a stubby pencil and a little black book from a messy pile of papers on the dash and asked us for the names of our next of kin. All I could think of was Heather at home with a houseful of hungry kids (more about that later). What would she ever do if we went down in flames?

The pilot revved up the engine and began a slow taxi onto the lake as I began with the Hail Marys—and I'm not even Catholic. Tony had his compass and map out trying to look nonchalant about it all. However, the beads of sweat forming on his forehead and his crossed fingers which he tried to hide under the map were sure giveaways.

We picked up speed and headed for the opposite shore with the feeble old lad huffing and puffing while he pulled mightily back on the stick. Were we going to make it? Not a chance. Not this try, anyway. Back we went to the dock for one more try, and still no lift off. Finally, he called up all the horses he had and torqued up the old clunker to its limit. The only thing that wasn't banging and shaking was the generator. It was too heavy. We barely made it over the treeline on the third try, as the songbirds and squirrels in the treetops scattered for cover.

As previously arranged, we were waiting for the plane to pick us up at 4:00 p.m. on the southeast shore of Mijin Lake. This time the plane wasn't loaded, but that old bush pilot sure as hell was. We could smell the booze coming from the cockpit even before the plane set down on the lake. The old bugger must have spent his whole day ferrying awestruck American fishermen from Sault Ste. Marie, Michigan, into Hawk Junction country.

The last thing I remember prior to falling asleep in the foremen's shack at Mile 100 that night was Tony on his knees at the end of his bunk before jumping into bed. Now I lay me down to sleep. Lord, take me through to breakfast.

Our next trip was a long walk on a hot summer day starting a few miles from Highway 17 and heading in an easterly direction toward the railway track. I can recall that we had an early breakfast at Mile 100 and left our truck alongside the highway as the sun peeked over the horizon. We walked all day, up and down hills, back and forth, without making much progress in distance due to the difficult terrain.

Around four o'clock we were exhausted and decided to call it a day. On our way back to the truck, we stopped for a rest. As we sat quietly on a fallen tree beside a beaver dam, we spotted a curious-looking clearing across the swamp in front of us. There was something unusual about the opening's irregular shape and appearance. We pulled out the aerial photographs to have a closer examination, after which our interest was aroused even more. The clearing didn't look natural. It seemed man-made. And since there hadn't been any previous logging in the area, what could it be?

We couldn't shake the Tom Sawyer and Huckleberry Finn spirit of a new adventure, which made us tingle with boyish excitement. We had to go and see for ourselves, even though it would take us a couple of hours off our course. And that would mean warmed-over beans, cold raisin pie, and a grumpy cook back at the Mile 100 camp.

As we walked around the edge of the swamp in the direction of the clearing, Tony recalled having heard from some of the locals in the Wawa area that many years before there had been some surface gold exploration activity in areas south of town. Maybe we would stumble on the remains of an old mining camp and the ghosts of some hard-rock gold miners. Sure enough, that is what we found.

We had arrived on Treasure Island and were like a couple of little boys thrashing around under the tree on Christmas morning. It was obvious there hadn't been any activity for five years or more. We couldn't believe what had been left behind. There were two large collapsed tents with wooden floors, a dozen single bunks, and opened and unopened cases of axes, shovels, picks, and other tools. The remains of a cookery tent was fully equipped with two kitchen ranges, pots and pans, kitchen utensils and much more.

We had come so far; there would have to be a reward for our discovery. We were not going to go home empty-handed. Under the rotting canvas of the former tents were two small, steel, barrel stoves, ideal for a workshop or a garage. Each stove was the size of a couple of twenty-pound propane barbeque tanks. We each strapped a stove onto our backs and also tied on some pieces of plastic sheeting. It was getting late, we were tired, and since the stoves were heavy, it soon became obvious that we couldn't carry them out to the truck that day.

We selected an identifiable location from the aerial photos about a half mile from the eventual location of the O'Connor Road and cached the stoves under some spruce trees, carefully covering them with the plastic and a few spruce branches. Some day when the road was finished, we would return and recover our treasures. But we never did. And as far as I know, the stoves are still where we left them. However, I know that Tony and I could still find them. Maybe some day when we enter our second childhoods, we'll fetch our boots from the closet and return for a nostalgic walk into our past.

Some time later we learned more details about the exploration work from the park superintendent, Red Montgomery. A fly-by-night gold exploration company working on behalf of a company that owned the mineral rights had moved into areas in the park suspected of containing gold deposits. They set up the camp we found and moved their supplies in on a trail they cut through the bush. A small bulldozer pulled stone boats loaded with their gear into the camp where a dozen or more men and their cook stayed.

The work consisted of surface exploration only. There was no drilling involved. The bulldozer scraped away the overburden to expose the bedrock, and the men used picks and shovels to sort through the surface rubble in search of gold. The dozer was the key to the job. It worked continuously, hauling supplies and bulldozing potential deposit locations.

One day the bulldozer sufffered a major break in its final drive. The penny stock market couldn't finance repairs to the dozer or a replacement, so that was the end of the job. The next day the crew walked out to Highway 17 carrying only personal gear in packsacks on their backs. Everything else remained behind, including the bulldozer, which was left where it had broken down about a mile from the camp. Red didn't know the exact location of the abandoned dozer, and as far as he knew it had never been repaired or recovered.

So there you have it; to this day, somewhere in the bowels of Lake Superior Park, there are two hidden steel barrel stoves and a rusty old bulldozer with a ghost or two wisping around it on dark nights. Doesn't that make your juices flow? It still does for me. And not once since that day have I even been tempted to purchase a single share of mining exploration penny stock.

After substantial work on western sections of the branch road to the highway, it was now time to explore the railroad end of the project. We had been told that there was an abandoned shack near O'Connor, which at one time was used by Algoma Central Railway section workers, and occasionally by moose hunters. It was equipped with a stove and beds and was apparently in pretty good shape. We made plans to spend three days there early one November. We boarded the morning train in the Soo and asked the conductor to drop us off at the shack.

With a strange and curious look on his face, he asked, "Are you really intending to stay in that shack?" When we replied, "yes," I caught the trace of a crooked little smile as he turned his head in the direction of a fellow trainman. The couched smile didn't register until after the train had slowed down to let us off.

When unloading passengers at non-scheduled stops, the train would not stop. Instead, it would slow down enough to allow the passengers to jump safely out of the baggage car. The gear was then passed, or, more accurately, thrown out the door. We had to be nimble.

As we picked up our packsacks, we began to assess our new home, which was less than fifteen feet from the track. The first impression was that the wind from a fast-moving train could blow it to smithereens. A sinking lost-at-sea feeling set in as the train disappeared out of sight around a curve. Right away, we knew we were facing an adventure in survival, and it was going to be a cold one. A real challenge on a dark near-winter afternoon in desolate ACR country.

Traces of snow on the floor greeted us as we opened the door, which hung limply to one side on a broken hinge. The stove had three legs, a squirrel's nest and a hole in the bottom, while a couple of sections of stovepipe lay crumpled in a corner. The only stars that our O'Connor Hilton could boast were ones that would be visible through the hole in the roof on a clear night.

The wire bunks had gaping holes which some desperate hunter had tried to repair with rusted haywire. One bed had two legs which had fallen through the rotting floor. Two out of the three windows were broken. Empty beer bottles were strewn everywhere. It was a mess!

"What we need in this situation, Brent, is to develop ourselves a good home-improvement plan," Tony sighed, as he lit up a cigarette and sat down to relax on an old wooden dynamite box that lay upside down in a corner.

"You're right, Tony," I replied, while reaching into a packsack to fetch a bottle of "Brown Jug," part of our emergency ration, packed for such an occasion.

We planned and planned, then planned some more. Finally, we had a plan and were in perfect shape to execute it. It was now time to get to work. The stove was propped up with rocks, and the windows and the hole in the roof were repaired with sheets of plastic that we had brought with us. Spruce boughs were cut and laid out as mattresses on our dilapidated bunks. A new hole was made in a wall about five feet from the floor to accommodate a shortened stovepipe configuration.

There was good water in a small, nearby creek, but the lack of good firewood close by forced us to burn green poplar that first night. By suppertime, we had a fire going in the stove, but could barely see each other across the room because of the dense smoke. There was more smoke coming out of the cracks in the stove than there was going out the pipe. We could only dream of those two little steel barrel stoves that lay in the bush a million miles way. Our eyes watered and our lungs burned.

We fried up some steaks and mushrooms with baked potatoes, and did a little more planning after supper. After the Little Brown Jug was emptied, it was converted into a candelabra for our makeshift kitchen table. Then it was off to bed, but not to sleep. The smoke was so thick that we had to let the fire go out before we could doze off, about 1:00 a.m. We had good sleeping bags, so keeping warm was not a problem.

Then the world ended. It started with a low rumbling off in the distance and climaxed with a fast-moving freight train ripping through the living room of our trackside residence. We didn't see him, but could only imagine the sight of a wide-eyed engineer pulling on the steam whistle, and roaring with laughter like a damned fool as he sped past us. By the time we had tumbled out of our bunks and stumbled out the door, we could only shake angry fists at a faint light in the caboose as the train faded out of sight and the lonesome whistle wailed into the distance of the black Algoma night.

"Casey Jones probably noticed the smoke coming through the walls and just couldn't resist the temptation to blow a couple of loggers out of bed. I can't believe the roof didn't come down on top of us," Tony growled. "I'll bet that's the first time since the track was laid that a train whistle has ever been blown in this godforsaken place. But we'll fix him tomorrow night. He won't wake us up the second time."

And sure enough, he didn't wake us the next night. Because, we didn't go to bed. There we were as the engine's headlight peeked around the bend, waiting for him on our doorstep in our designer combination underwear, boots, and hard hats. As he passed, blowing on his whistle again, we could see him looking down at us in surprise while I swung an axe over my head with a threatening motion at the engine. An excited Tony pumped a Pierre Trudeau one-finger salute at him with both hands.

"Yes, sir, we sure fixed that whistle-happy puppy. Likely scared the hell out of him," Tony laughed, as we climbed back into our toasty bunks.

We stayed at O'Connor for three nights and were able to find good firewood and patch up the stove and stovepipes. By the end of our stay, the shack was quite livable. As we flagged down the train for our return trip to the Soo, we reflected on our time at O'Connor. We had made good progress with our road location work and agreed that the comfort of our home away from home was a result of our *Better Homes and Gardens* planning skills.

The following spring we were back on the train once again to check out another section of the road. This time the trip took us to White Spruce Lake, which would be our work base for five days. White Spruce was a remote lake about a mile west of the Sand River and fourteen miles from Highway 17. It was small, less than a mile long, and reportedly chock-full of speckled trout. There were no designated campsites on the lake and the rugged, mainly uphill, portage trail from river to lake was not maintained by park staff.

It was in early May with patches of snow still prevalent in swamps and lower slopes, so we were well prepared with a good tent and warm clothing. Tony and I had similar preferences in food and visited a downtown deli in Sault Ste. Marie one day to load up on hot salamis, ripe cheese, and rye bread. A good supply of flour and butter was added for the much anticipated feasts of trout. We were not to be disappointed. However, as some severe portaging was anticipated, the Little Brown Jug was left behind to lighten the load. Besides, there wouldn't be any renovation projects on this trip.

We were dropped off on a section of track near the south end of Sand Lake. Once again, the train didn't stop, but slowed down enough to allow the trainman to slide our canoe out the baggage-car door to our outstretched arms. Next came the packsacks, which we caught as we ran down the side of the track to keep up with the train. Luckily, we hadn't packed eggs, knowing that we would be fielding our bags like a tight end running down the sidelines towards the end zone.

We paddled down the stunningly beautiful Sand River for a few miles, enjoying its treasures of rippling rapids and quiet sections of meandering crystal-clear water. At one point, we laid the paddles across the gunnels and sat motionless and speechless as the gentle current carried us downstream, passing under a huge overhanging yellow birch tree and a rock outcropping covered by a multi-coloured blanket of moss. The birds were singing quietly as their day ended, and the air was brisk and fresh, so much so that there was not a black fly or mosquito in sight. Pretty hard to imagine a man getting well paid for this kind of work, not to mention the free room and board and outstanding trout fishing.

Then I did something that proved to be most untimely, and certainly not profitable at the time. I turned around to Tony, who was paddling in the stern, and said, "Tony, I know you are a busy man, and I have been waiting a long time to get you alone, away from the nagging telephones and those damned accountants standing in your doorway pestering you for another production forecast. I wonder if we could take a few minutes to talk about a possible raise in my wages?"

Tony's response will remain unrecorded. It will forever be for my ears only.

However, the pleasure was quick to disappear and the work to start when we left the river and struggled to manhandle our canoe and supplies up to the lake over the rugged terrain. The trail was barely visible through the dense bush, although we could see the occasional old axe blaze where someone before us had worked to clear the way. We took turns carrying the canoe over our heads, but because of the thick undergrowth, there were long stretches where we each had to take one end of the canoe and muscle it through the brush.

It was in late afternoon, and we felt adventure and excitement when we approached the shore of that little jewel of a lake. The sight was serene and absolutely breathtaking. The bow of the loaded canoe was eased into the gentle water, and as we left the shore, had the fishing rods out and the hooks baited. Our supper was caught and on a string before the paddles were even wet, and well before we knew where we would be spending the night.

For the next half hour, we paddled slowly around the lake, looking for a level spot to make camp. Since there were no cleared or marked campsites on the lake, we hoped to find a spot where somebody else had carved out a campsite before us. The shoreline was quite steep, and just when we were beginning to think we would have to find a site inland, we sighted something extraordinary nestled amongst the trees in a small bay near the outlet of the lake. We pulled the canoe up on shore and walked up the bank to investigate.

Now I have visited Stonehenge, the Magic Kingdom, and Westminister Abbey and, believe me, not one of those man-made creations was any more impressive than what we accidentally found that day near the shore of White Spruce Lake. It was a small cedar-shake cabin about seven feet long and four feet wide. But it was not just an ordinary cabin. It had been built on posts or stilts, and stood proudly against the background of the surrounding pines. The cabin peered down at us from a height of about six feet above ground level.

As we looked up at the cabin in amazement, it appeared to be in excellent shape with a solid roof, a secured front door, and a small front verandah, all constructed from cedar shakes. The stilts were wrapped their full length in tin, with pointed spike-ends sticking out about every six inches. At first glance, we could see that this was intended to keep animals from accessing the cabin. It also had the effect of preventing us from reaching the cabin.

We looked around for a small tree that we could cut down to lean against the structure to enable us to climb up. About thirty feet away, hidden behind a large pine tree, we found a crude ladder, which was obviously for that purpose. Once again, we were overcome with that Tom Sawyer and Huckleberry Finn feeling of finding a remote mining camp or exploring a hidden cave.

Tony was the first to scramble up the ladder to have a look, and as he did, I could see the cabin swaying a little from the effect of his weight.

Tony stood upright on the verandah, opened the door, and disappeared inside, while I waited anxiously below for his report.

"You're not going to believe this," he shouted back down to me. "No need to unpack the tent. There is a stove in here and two bunks. The only things missing are the chocolate mints on the pillows. Come up and have a look."

Further examination revealed two separate compartments, or storage cupboards, with doors opening on to the verandah. In one was an assortment of dried food, such as rolled oats and rice. In the other, a supply of dry and finely split firewood. Above the front door, some signage had been carved into the cedar indicating that this was a "Snowshoe Club" cabin, and that visitors were welcome to its use, asking that, if used, the cache of food and wood be replenished. The cedar-shake roof had a plastic liner and there was a small open window, which could be shut completely with a wooden slider. Above the window was another sign that read, "This cabin is airtight: always open the window slightly while sleeping."

Both bunks were made of cedar shake with a natural, rounded shape to fit the occupant's contours. The bottom bunk was stationary, while the top bunk was hinged and tied to the roof to provide headroom. There was still only enough room for two men to stand up, but at very close quarters, nose-to-nose, so to speak. A small candle sat on the only table next to the head of the bottom bunk.

It was the small steel stove that intrigued us the most. It was the size of a gallon syrup can with a tiny hinged door; a two-inch metal pipe was the chimney. The stove was loaded with dry wood and birch bark.

As we sat down on the bunk and looked around our lodgings for the next four nights, we could not help make the comparison between this cabin and the "shack on the track." What good fortune! There would be no need for a planning session that night.

Our thoughts continued while trying to imagine who would build such an amazing structure and why. The design was simple and functional in providing shelter for one or two people in this wild and remote country. The workmanship was very neat and precise. We marvelled at the fact that, for the most part, the cabin was built from materials obtained in the bush, namely the cedar shakes and cedar poles. The only supplies needed to be portaged into the site were nails, tin for the stilts, a roll of plastic, and the stove and stovepipe.

After our supper of freshly fried trout, so fresh that the fish curled up in the frying pan while cooking, we retired early. It had been a long, but very satisfying day. A coin was flipped for the bottom bunk, and Tony won. Served me right for hassling him over a pay raise, when under these circumstances a cut in wages would have been more appropriate.

Our cabin was so small that when the top bunk was lowered into the sleep position, there was no room to get undressed inside while standing up. So I waited outside on the verandah while Tony undressed and climbed into his bunk. A thirty-below night in February would have presented a challenge for that short wait on the verandah.

After we finally bedded down, we immediately realized that when one or the other of us rolled over in bed, the whole cabin swayed. This was a source of great amusement, and we laughed ourselves to sleep that night, miles away from the torment of a train whistle.
I have slept in Toronto's Royal York and Ottawa's Chateau Laurier, but neither provided me with a better night's sleep than was enjoyed that night on White Spruce Lake.

Tony Vorlicek on the shore of White Spruce Lake, Lake Superior Park: "Will that be the buffet, or would you like to order from the menu?"

We woke up to a cold morning around the freezing point, so Tony lit the candle and within ten minutes the cabin was comfortable. A fire in the stove would have made it too warm. In fact, the stove wasn't used once during our stay, as we fried our fish over an open fire each night.

We worked long hours while we were there and only needed about fifteen minutes of fishing each evening to catch our breakfast and supper supply for the next day. It was a bushman's dream come true and for me an experience unequalled before or since!

When we left White Spruce, we both vowed to return. Maybe Tony and I will do that someday and check on our stoves at the same time. That will be a nostalgia tour to beat all, but we had better put the plan to action and soon—before we find ourselves in wheelchairs in Slumber Rest Manor, huddled around the piano singing, "You are my sunshine, my only sunshine."

When we returned to our regular life back home, we talked often of the experience and committed ourselves to finding out more about the individual or individuals who had erected the cabin. The information we were able to obtain from some park staff members was sketchy and described an elderly, eccentric gentleman from Michigan, who had built three similar cabins in the park. He would come by himself to stay for extended periods, particularly in the winter months, travelling by snowshoes from one cabin to another. He apparently wrote of his solitary experiences for various outdoor life magazines in the U.S.

It wasn't until about twenty-five years later that I was fortunate to receive more information about our unusual and interesting host, and it came to me quite unexpectedly. Our good friend and neighbour, Marian Patterson, who lived across the street from us in Pembroke, had two visitors one day. Robert Gunn and Kathleen Naluzny were friends of her son, Jeff, and at the time were employed in Lake Superior Park: Kathleen at the park's interpretative centre and Robert in the maintenance department.

Marian had known of my work in the park and invited Heather and me over to meet these young people. We had an enjoyable time exchanging stories about the park, and I described the White Spruce Lake adventure with some enthusiasm. They were fascinated by the story and unaware of the existence of the cabin(s), but promised to research the matter upon their return to work.

A few weeks later, Marian came over with an envelope containing copies of correspondence between the Department of Lands and Forests' chief ranger in Wawa and the builder of the cabin, Mr. Les Perine of Michigan. The letters mainly outlined concerns Mr. Perine had with vandalism problems at one of his cabins. The package also included sketches and floor plans. The cabin that we stayed in was constructed in 1954, the year after the Queen's coronation, and was named Buckingham Palace by Mr. Perine.

The following is a memo dated October 30, 1969, from Park Superintendent E. M. (Red) Montgomery to the Wawa Chief Ranger of the Department of Lands and Forests.

> Mr. Perine was located on the Sand River when I first came to Sand Lake Headquarters in 1950.
>
> Apparently prior to moving the so called Snowshoe Club to Sand River he was located on the Montreal River before the first dam was constructed by the Great Lakes Power Co. at the A.C.R. Railway Bridge.
>
> Through my acquaintance with Mr. Perine I found out that he had been a research engineer with General Motors of Detroit, travelled worldwide with no ties or obligations, but enjoyed getting away in the bush by himself and never was a fisherman or a hunter.
>
> To my knowledge Mr. Perine built 3 cabins, #1 located on Sand Lake, #2 on White Spruce Lake, and #3 I never did see, but it was supposed to be along the Sand River. He spent considerable time in the area, would arrive Sand Lake late August and would leave the early part of November. He would return late January and leave again in early March.
>
> Mr. Perine always talked about his Snowshoe Club but to my knowledge except in one instance when another man did visit him for a day, only he was the entire club.
>
> As far as authority or right to construct these cabins, to my knowledge there never was any permission granted.
>
> In fact I was very surprised to hear that he was still around, this is the first I have heard of him for several years. Any time that I had occasion to visit his cabin there never was any supply of food around, instead he ate mostly dried fruits and cracked wheat cereal.

It has been almost forty years since Tony and I stayed in that little cabin in the sky. And Mr. Perine has been "down for much longer than that" (an old expression that comes to me from Jessie Morrison and Eleanor Hammond of Dunany, Quebec, to mark someone passing away.)

In the event we don't make it back to White Spruce, I like to think that the little cabin has not been reduced to an unrecognizable rubble. Rather, some worthy fishermen or concerned park staff members have maintained

Tony Vorlicek resting while waiting for an overdue Algoma Central "GO" train, Sand Lake, Lake Superior Park.

it somehow. Even though the cabin may not still be standing under the gentle whispering pines, the site is certainly deserving of some special protective status. If it was a hawk's nest, a heron rookery, or a native meeting place, there would be no question about that.

(While reliving the wonder of the White Spruce cabin, I recently talked to some of my former Weyerhaeuser friends and was pleased to hear that since our initial discovery of the cabin, Tony had returned to the site, as did Roy Perkins, Paul Nenonen, and Gordie Hoffman. There may have been others. Roy Perkins provided a photo of himself near a tent that had been pitched beside the cabin. He was there timber cruising and explained that, at that time, the cabin was too unsteady to be used.)

After I left Weyerhaeuser in 1975 to return to work in Algonquin Park, the O'Connor Road was eventually constructed from the highway to about a mile east of White Spruce Lake. It never did reach the ACR, as originally planned, due to a natural science issue over unique glacial deposits between the Sand River and the track. Harvesting operations on the road lasted for only two years, and logging in the park began to wind down forever.

The loss of Lake Superior Park was a serious setback to Weyerhaeuser's Sault Ste. Marie operation, so in the mid 1980s, the forest industry giant packed its bags and headed back out west. (The operation was sold to G. W. Martin Lumber Ltd. and continued to operate on a reduced scale for awhile. Since then, there have been other owners who struggled to survive; presently, only the sawmill continues to run. The veneer mill and flooring plant no longer exist.)

The environmentalists had won the battle, sending some of my old logger friends flocking to the city, licking their wounds on their way to the Algoma Steel's employment office to work liked caged animals in the shadows of a blazing blast furnace hidden from the fresh Algoma air and gentle rays of the sun. Not to mention the blinding blizzards, the numbing forty-below mornings, and the dark swarms of mosquitos and black flies. Kind of sad, really.

In the summer of 2007, Heather and I drove across Canada, and on our way through Lake Superior Park, I watched closely for recognizable landmarks. It had been thirty-one years since I had walked the side-hills of that beautiful place, and I was excited. I could barely pick out the entrance into Camp 100, but, upon finding it, walked in to look at the former site, which by now was a clearing returning to its natural forested state.

There were no buildings, only memories. Memories of college girls selling *Woman's Day* magazines to a bunkhouse full of loggers, of a dumb logging superintendent trying to show a seasoned mechanic how to change the spark plugs in a diesel engine, and of men gathered in Art's Place after supper for a news update.

A tear may have formed, I'm not sure. It sure felt like it.

I drove right by the entrance of the O'Connor Road onto the highway and had to turn the car around to find it. There was no more road there; just a rusty steel gate stretching across a breached trail barely wide enough for two moose to follow each other in single file. And after all that hard work, nothing but the hidden remains of two steel barrel stoves, the drone of a far-off train whistle, and the ghosts of toughened loggers flitting about in a little cabin on stilts.

But by the time we reached Wawa, I had cheered myself up. Because I had something that a stroke of a pen behind a heavy door at Queen's Park could never take away from me. I still had the memories and the friendships of those days gone by, of the chats we had while lying in our bunks at night or sitting around a campfire picking our teeth with a sharpened spruce twig after a feast of fresh trout. I can smell the woodsmoke still.

# Chapter 12: A Tome of Tony's Time in the Bush

*"I swear that in Lake Superior Park, the creeks all run up hill."*
—Antonin (Tony) Vorlicek, Woods Manager, Weyerhaeuser

What better opportunity than now to share some of Tony Vorlicek's recollections and in his own words, more or less, as near as I can recall them . . .

Mile 100 threw everything at you: two-foot deep, twenty-four hour snowfalls; blinding blizzards; scattered timber; and an unfriendly but beautiful landscape so chopped up with a jumble of rocks and waterways that it would make you want to howl at the moon and spit out peas. The sweet dreams that I have about the many weekends that I canoed and fished in Lake Superior Park are more than matched by the nightmares I have had over the years of logging that jigsaw puzzle.

Stan Olsen was our woods manager for a while and I worked for him as logging superintendent. He was an American coming to Sault Ste. Marie with considerable practical experience gained from working on Weyerhaeuser's west coast logging operations. He was a good man, always keen to go to the bush to have a look at future logging areas.

It was a beautiful sunny winter morning when Stan and I left Mile 100 camp shortly after breakfast to walk some new area near Stovepipe Lake. We were on snowshoes and made good time in the morning. But that changed quickly around noon when a very heavy snowfall began. The snowfall was so dense that we could barely see ten feet ahead—with snowflakes as big as gypsy moths. We took turns breaking trail, and I can recall Stan was wearing a red parka mackinaw that day. There were times when he was ahead that all I could make out was a slow-moving, faint red blur.

We continued walking toward Stovepipe Lake, expecting that it was only a brief squall coming in from Lake Superior. But by two o'clock, the snow had not let up and the temperature had warmed drastically, maybe six degrees or more. Now the snow was so wet that our snowshoes began to sink about ten inches into the snow. Each time we lifted our shoes out of the snow for the next step, it felt like we were carrying another eight pounds. Our steps became shorter and slower. We were sweating like bulls, and then the temperature turned very cold as quickly as it had turned warmer earlier. That had the effect of cooling us off and, along with our wet underclothes, we became chilled. Things were looking bad so we decided to head out to our jeep.

Our route was a loop, so we couldn't walk back on the original trail without adding substantial distance to the return trip. We had to continue to break trail and were quickly becoming severely exhausted. And still the snow continued. Darkness started to set in shortly after four o'clock and we were still a couple of miles from the jeep. What should we do? Should we stop and build a fire and a lean-to for the night or continue to struggle on?

We were in a hardwood bush of yellow birch and maple, and there were no spruce, balsam, or cedar trees close by to provide boughs to build a shelter. We decided that it would take too much of our remaining energy to find the needed softwood, so we carried on. By the time we crossed the ice on Coldwater Creek, we were walking in total darkness and had to use a cigarette lighter to check our compass bearings as we walked. We couldn't stop walking to look at the compass—we were too cold. A haunting feeling of panic spurred us on.

Our jeep was parked on the top of a hill, and finally we reached the bottom of the hill. We were now encouraged, knowing that there was only another gruelling half mile to go. The excruciating pain of our last few steps quickly faded as we sighted the ghostlike outline of that precious little yellow jeep, waiting patiently for our return.

The rugged, four-wheel drive jeep plunged bravely through a foot of freshly fallen snow as we headed out to the highway and safety. When we arrived at the highway, we faced a three-foot high pile of snow which had been pushed up by the highway snowplow.

I was driving, and I can recall Stan blurting out, "Give 'er shit, Tony. You have to get us through that pile of snow because I just don't have the strength to even pick up a shovel."

We made it on to the highway on the second try and were back at camp shortly after nine to be greeted by some anxious crew members, who were getting ready to come looking for us. Boy, were they relieved to see us as we stumbled into the foremen's shack, as was the thoughtful cook who had our supper warming in the oven.

Scotty Jamieson was bulldozing a winter road on the same day that Stan and I had our adventure and fell victim to the same snowfall. He was building the road from the highway into a new cutting area and had started in the morning with fresh construction from the highway entrance. [Unlike the current practice of pre-cutting the right-of-way with chainsaws and skidders, in those days, the dozer operator followed axe-blazes or flagging tape on trees on the centre line and used the blade to clear the trees and debris from the road surface ahead. It wasn't a very efficient or orderly method, but that was how it was done then.]

Scotty's forward visibility was limited by the storm so, from time to time, he had to stop the dozer and walk ahead to find the blazes. Scotty was a first-class bulldozer operator, but had never laid claim to being a bushman. Laying out the road was somebody else's job. Scotty's commitment was: "Show me the way to go and I'll build you a road there."

So with the increasing snowfall, the inevitable happened. Somehow, Scotty got off the blazes for a short section of road, but kept on dozing with the expectation that he would soon come across the blazes again . . . somewhere, that is, between his location and the ACR track.

As he pushed and scraped while rubbing the driving snow from his bleary eyes, he was thrilled to be making such good time. Finally the dozer inched up over a slight incline, and Scotty could see a large clearing ahead through the cloud of snow. What good fortune! Maybe now he would be back on to the blazes.

"Well, I'll be damned," Scotty moaned, as his dozer inched up onto the shoulder of the Trans Canada Highway, not far from where he had started.

Scotty had created a truck-driver's dream: drive in with an empty truck through one entrance and drive out loaded through the other—just like the road into the Caysee Lake Campground. Reports from the bunkhouse that night were that a melancholy mood had replaced Scotty's usual cheerfulness as he sat in the darkness on the edge of his bunk staring blankly into space. "Aye, but it's been a bleak day, another one of those 'I can't get there from here days.'"

What a great guy he was! He did the work of two men and was always willing to go the extra mile, even if it occasionally took him out to the highway.

I recall one summer at Mile 67, about five o'clock, when I was driving in from the bush in time for supper at the camp. I passed a branch road that Scotty was building and decided to drive in to see how he was making out.

He revved down the dozer while I jumped up on the track to talk to him. "Tony," he said, "I forgot my watch in the bunkhouse this morning. Is it lunchtime yet?" And that pretty much sums up old Scotty's dedication to his job.

Winter logging conditions in Lake Superior Park and at Mile 67 were really quite unbelievable and had to be seen to be appreciated. Sometimes, extra snow shovellers were hired to shovel around the stump of the trees being cut, and D6 bulldozers were used to plow skid trails to individual trees.

The question had often been asked by Weyerhaeuser's Tacoma executives: If the conditions were that harsh in the wintertime, why not log in the park in the non-winter months and go someplace else in the winter? There were two answers to that question. Firstly, the park was an important source of high-value, yellow birch veneer logs to supply the Soo veneer mill, thus justifying the burden of excessive logging costs; secondly, it was clear that the environmental influence was leading to the eventual termination of logging in the park, so we negotiated a deal with the Ontario Department of Lands and Forests that bought us a few more years in the park.

The agreement was that we would log there in winter months only, thus alleviating any real or perceived conflict with summer recreational use. It seemed like a good deal at the time, but all it really did was prolong the agony of logging under near impossible conditions.

We faced constant labour turnover. Loggers wouldn't work as pieceworkers because of the tough conditions and low productivity, and were paid by the hour or day. Many resisted living in a bush camp so far away from home. And, most of all, it was brutal, dangerous work. Every Monday morning there were new faces in camp, many of them not fully skilled and requiring training. All of us, especially the logging supervisors, were pushed to the limits to keep things going.

I can recall in 1962 on New's Year Eve when my wife, Mary, and I were planning a quiet evening at home. I received a phone call from Glen Sundstrom, who was our road construction foreman at the time. That afternoon he had been called by the bull cook (or choreboy) from Mile 100 to say that everything was plugged with snow at the camp—it had snowed everyday since the day before Christmas.

Glen went on to say, "The log haul is scheduled to start at 6:00 a.m. on January 2nd, and I can't reach anybody to come and help me open up the roads. All the lads must be out celebrating. Can you come with me, Tony?"

So I kissed Mary goodnight and wished her a Happy New Year, and jumped into my truck and headed for Mile 100. I got there around 9:00 p.m. to find Glen cleaning out the camp yard with a front-end loader. When that was done we went to the bush. Glen started up an old D8 bulldozer and I climbed onto a D6 dozer. We pushed snow all night and well into the next day. There were some hills that had to be sanded, but we were so bushed that we just flopped into our bunks and went right to sleep. The road crew would have to sand the hills when they arrived.

On the morning of January 2nd, we expected to be awakened before dawn by the roar of log trucks in the camp yard. But not to be! Instead, all we heard was the old choreboy shovelling freshly fallen snow from the walkway in front of the foremen's shack. There wasn't even a trace of a log truck until the following morning. By that time there was another six or eight inches of snow on the ground and a few more points on my blood-pressure scale.

Whenever the people from Tacoma reviewed financial statements for operations at Mile 100, all hell would break loose. And that is why creative accountants were worth their weight in gold to us. I remember one time a whiz-kid vice president from Tacoma came for a visit. He was going to show us how to tame the lion.

Early one winter morning, I picked him up at his hotel for the two-hour drive to Mile 100. The minute he opened the door to get into my truck, the bullshit started. It was a blow-by-blow explanation of the excellence of Weyerhaeuser's logging systems in the great states of Washington, Oregon, and Arkansas, not to mention the Philippines and South America. His Weyerhaeuser system could log on the moon and make it pay. He couldn't understand why we were having so much difficulty.

"I'm sure I'll spot something that you boys have overlooked," he offered. It was non-stop for two hours. By the time we reached the camp, I was ready to throw up.

I stopped at the camp to find out where the log trucks were. Sonny Dugas was the only truck in the bush at the time, and I knew where I would meet him on his way out loaded. Now was the perfect time for me to put on my own show and even things up a bit.

It was like driving through a narrow snow tunnel shaped by eight- to ten-foot snowbanks. I knew the road well and stepped on the gas a bit. If this guy was going to show us how to log in this country, we shouldn't be wasting any of his valuable time. Besides, he had a plane to catch back home that night.

We skidded around a couple of corners, and after a nerve-racking, triple-axel bank shot, I glanced over at my passenger. He was sitting on the edge of his seat with his fingernails dug into the dash of the truck. "Holy old shit," he screamed, "you should be building your roads a lot wider than this."

"Wide roads are too costly for the low yields of timber per mile in this area," I replied quietly. That was one on the board for me.

Finally, we arrived at a log landing. He got out and looked around at the landing and up at the massive mountain that we were logging. "Where are all the men?" he asked.

"There is a cutter over there," I said, pointing to a nearby yellow birch tree with snow flying up from a hole in the snow around the base.

We walked over and looked down to see Johnnie Boissonneault shovelling snow away from the stump. In a minute, we heard the muffled sound of his chainsaw and could see a puff of blue smoke rising out of the hole. Next came Johnnie jumping out of the hole as the tree fell in the opposite direction. He smiled at us as he slid into his snowshoes, grabbed the shovel and chainsaw, and looked around for the next tree. My colleague wasn't shaking his head, but I knew he wanted to.

Then he spotted a distant D6 bulldozer crawling around on top of the hill. "Don't tell me you're building roads way the hell up there in the clouds," he said.

I explained that because of the severe snow depths, we had to build skid trails to each tree to provide access for the skidders. It was time to score another point, so I suggested, "Let's walk up the main skid trail and have a look."

After ten minutes walking up the steep hill from the landing, he was huffing and puffing like a black bear in heat. Probably had smoked too many cigars while visiting Cuba to show them how to log the Weyerhaeuser way. He played out on me half way up the hill and that was the end of my logging lesson for the day. It was time to catch a plane.

There was very little conversation on the drive back to the Soo, and when I dropped him off at the airport, he said to me, simply, "Just do the best you can, Tony." And I never saw or heard from the man after that day.

Drinking in or around the camps was strictly forbidden, and anyone caught doing so was sent on a one-way trip to town on the next log truck. That's not to say there wasn't a mickey or two hidden under a mattress, here or there, that the foremen weren't aware of. In any event, drinking in the camps was never a problem. The men were there to log, not to play.

However, the annual Christmas party was the one exception to the rule. On the evening of the last day of work before the Christmas break, the cooks at each camp prepared a full-course turkey dinner, complete with stuffing and plum pudding. For some, it would be a better meal than what they would get at home in a few days. In the afternoon, I loaded up my truck with booze in the Soo and dropped half the load off at Mile 67 and the balance at Mile 100. After the meal was finished, the boys got into it with the foremen keeping a close eye on things, for as long as they were capable of doing so. I didn't stay around for the festivities, because after the first beer, the men would be telling me how much more money they would need to be paid before coming back to work after the New Year.

When the party was over in the wee hours, the men went to bed, and after they sobered up with a few gallons of coffee at breakfast, they were driven in the crew bus safely back to town. There were never any fights or uprisings that I'm aware of, with the exception of one incident; it was reported at breakfast one year that somebody got mad at Ben Harvey and shoved a rifle barrel in his face. However, as the story unfolded, there was some controversy over the details of the fracas.

When the crews arrived back to work after the holiday, the real story was heard from the apparent perpetrator: "All I did was point the choreboy's broom handle at Ben, nothing more," he chuckled.

The loggers worked hard under tough conditions and occasionally could get cranked up over the slightest issue. There is an example that comes to mind . . .

I left the office one day and was just sitting down to eat my supper at home when the phone rang. It was the camp foreman from Mile 100.

"I have a rebellion on my hands up here, Tony. The men are threatening not to go to work tomorrow," he said anxiously.

"Can't you sort it out yourself?" I asked.

"No, I've tried, but they want to see you," was the reply.

So, once again, I kissed Mary good night, jumped into my truck and headed up to the camp. When I arrived at the camp there was a committee waiting for me in the foremen's shack. They had a spokesman.

"What's the problem, boys?" I asked.

"The pies in the cookery are too small," the spokesman replied sternly.

"They are standard-sized pies," I pointed out.

"Yeah, but the slices are too small."

"Are they good pies?" I asked.

"For sure, they're good pies."

"Can you have as many pieces as you want?"

"Yeah, but the slices are too small."

As I looked around at the other crew members, I could see a few reluctant smiles starting to appear. "Just a minute," I said.

So I walked over to the cookery and told the cook, "Cut those damned pies into four pieces before the whole camp walks out on us."

I went back into the foremen's quarters and announced to the committee, "The problem is fixed, boys. You're going to have bigger pieces of pie from now on."

"Are there any other problems?" I asked them.

"Nope, everything is fine," was the reply.

So I went into the cookery, had a cup of coffee and a big piece of pie, fuelled up my truck, and drove home.

Those were some of the twists and turns that logging in Lake Superior Park served up, while at the same time not to suggest that operating at Mile 67 was a stroll through the park, because it wasn't. It was equally as tough. After all, it was just thirty-three miles down the road.

And the one important thing that I learned early on was to always have my truck fuelled up in the driveway ready to go, and be prepared to kiss Mary goodnight twenty-four hours every and any day.

# Chapter 13: Payback Time for Some Accountants

***"Never do what you say you are going to do, because that way there would be no variance from the forecast—and I would be out of a job."***

—A nameless Weyerhaeuser accountant

The high cost of logging in Algoma was a woods manager's nightmare, and, at the same time, an accountant's dream come true. Weyerhaeuser's Sault Ste. Marie office had almost as many accountants scurrying about as there were bulldozer operators and truck drivers in the bush operations. There were a lot of dollars to follow around, so these slick sleuths were everywhere in their neat sports jackets, designer ties, and nifty Soprano sunglasses.

Their days were filled completing forecasts and comparing today's actual to yesterday's estimate of what was supposed to happen today. Mao Zedong's motto was stamped on their foreheads: "If you are going to get into the forecasting business, make sure that you do it frequently."

Whenever I had the opportunity and there was a crowd around, I would tease them by describing a typical accountant's day: The first thing an accountant does when he comes to the office in the morning is sit down and forecast how many cups of coffee will be brewed in the office coffeemaker before the end of the day. The last thing he does before he goes home is to complete an actual consumption report, followed by a variance report and a few graphs, all of which are forwarded to everyone in the office with a notation, "Please review and provide comments within two days."

But I have to be clear. I have always appreciated my accountant colleagues, and, like the loggers I have worked with, have never met one I didn't like. Although on a couple of occasions, I had to take a second look. Reminds me of the old adage, "Show me a person that I don't like and that's the person I have to get to know better."

I will be the first to argue that a smart, practical accountant is an indispensable management resource, and I have been privileged to have worked with some outstanding ones. The reason that I am taking the liberty of roasting them on this occasion is that it will be my only opportunity to reciprocate for the endless times they dished up bad news to us struggling loggers. I do this with great respect and in the spirit of fun.

I can recall a day in the middle of December as being a particularly frenzied one with just about everything around me flying apart. The phone was smoking and there was a waiting room full of logging contractors with their tongues hanging out and their shirt sleeves rolled up.

Since I used to help Tony with production forecasts, accountant Claude Drolet approached me with a request for a first-quarter delivery forecast for log production in the New Year from the camp operations. I hurriedly completed the forecast as best I could, and, with a stroke of sarcasm reflecting a little impatience with the distraction, added a notation at the bottom of the spread sheet, "Regardless of how many 4-foot snowfalls there will be in January and February, the last load of logs for the season will be delivered into the Sault Ste. Marie log yard at 11:00 a.m on March 27th." And I signed it.

That was the last I thought of the matter until three months later on March 24th or 25th, when Claude jokingly reminded me of my prediction. That heads-up bean counter had either remembered or had made note of my silliness.

As it turned out, I had some work to do at Mile 100 on the 26th and discovered that the hauling operations were almost completed. There were a few loads, called calves, scattered at various locations throughout the job and were being picked up by a couple of trucks. (A "calf" or "calves" is truck-driver's terminology to describe a load that either had to be unloaded along the roadside because of the mechanical breakdown of the truck, or some other mishap. These loads were usually out on the main roads and were the last to be picked up at the end of the season, which in a typical year at Mile 100 was around the end of March.)

I stayed overnight at the camp on the 26th, and the next morning was driving back to Sault Ste. Marie. As I approached the Lighthouse Restaurant, I spotted Ab Hoffman's loaded truck in the parking lot. Suddenly, the bells rang and the lights came on. I knew what I had to do next. I stopped and went into the restaurant and found Ab having a coffee and talking to some other truckers.

I asked him when he expected to arrive in the Soo yard and he said, "If I push it, I will be there shortly after ten."

I explained the prediction I had made to Claude, and since Ab was one of the good guys and was also being paid by the hour, he accepted my offer of another coffee and order of toast, and agreed to come through the millyard gate at exactly 11:00 a.m., pulling on the air horn. Then I raced to the mill for the upcoming show.

At five-to-eleven, I rounded up Claude Drolet, Mac Backer, Ray McGuire, and a few others at the huge window overlooking the log yard. At precisely eleven o'clock, Ab appeared at the gate behind the wheel of his big yellow-and-black Mack truck loaded with logs. His horn was blasting, and he was waving out the window at us with both arms. He must have been steering the truck with his knees, but he was grinning as if crossing the finish line under the checkered flag at the Daytona 500.

"There you are, lads," I pointed out confidently, "as I predicted in December. That load you see is the last one for the season from Mile 100."

Of course they didn't need to know that there were another half dozen or so loads to come in over the next day or two. They had already returned to their desks to complete the actual-to-date and variance reports, so I didn't feel the need to provide any further information and disturb them as they worked on their latest updates.

# Chapter 14: Darting Off to Mattawa

***"Every good fishing lake in Algonquin Park is within walking distance, that is, if you have the time."***

—Clarence Clouthier, logging superintendent, expert bushman

An unknown writer once compared the span of a person's lifetime in relation to the age of our planet; it is little more than the flick of a firefly on a warm summer night or a puff of breath from a buffalo on a forty-below zero morning on the prairie. In a way that reflects our time in Mattawa—no longer than a quick glimpse of a firefly. But I wouldn't have missed it for the world.

But before darting off to Mattawa, I have a brief personal story to share.

Heather and I are looking forward to celebrating our fortieth wedding anniversary in October of 2008. More than four decades before, we met after both of us had experienced failed marriages. Each of us brought three children into a new family, and what makes it such a remarkable story, for me a least, is that the kids are so close in age. On our wedding day, the attendants were a nine-year-old girl, two seven-year-old boys, two six-year-old girls, and one five-year-old boy. We subsequently adopted each others' kids, and a year later on Halloween night, the family was treated to a baby girl.

When people who don't know us very well discover that there were six teenagers in our home for more than three years, they ask, "And how did you manage that?" Neither one of us has a clear answer for that question. But whatever the response happens to be on a given day, it always comes with a smile of satisfaction. Sometimes I'll sum it up this way, "Heather didn't buy bread by the loaf in those days—she bought it by the cord."

Were there any crises during that time? Only one that I can recall, and that was on the first morning after the expanded family had moved into our new house in Sault Ste. Marie. Thinking that our biggest problem was going to be one of economics, I jumped out of bed early one morning under the cover of darkness to mix up some powdered milk for breakfast and one of the kids caught me. The howls of protest could be heard in Soo, Michigan, and that was the end of that deception. To this day, every once in awhile, I will overhear one of them say, "Boy, we sure came up the hard way, during those tough times back in the Soo in the 1960s, when Dad tried to feed us powdered milk."

I was working as Weyerhaeuser's branch forester in the Sault Ste. Marie office one Friday morning in June of

1969, when the phone rang around 11:30 a.m. It was Jack Schikofsky, the general manager responsible for Weyerhaeuser's eastern Canadian operations. His office was located in our building, and he asked if I would come down to see him before lunch. I had that "something was up" feeling as I anxiously opened his door and sat down in front of a huge, intimidating desk.

Jack came right to the point, as was his custom. "Our operation at Mattawa is having serious problems and is losing money in a big way. If we don't turn things around quickly, those Yankee boys out in Tacoma, Washington, will soon be pulling the Mattawa pin off their map and throwing it away. I'm doing a major make-over in the mill and on the logging operation with a number of staffing changes. I want you to go there as our new logging manager—right away."

I picked up on the "right away" immediately, and after a few questions about salary and accommodation for my family and some more information about the operation of the Mattawa branch, I asked, "When would you like to have my decision, Jack?"

"I don't need to know right now. Are you going home for lunch?" he asked.

When I replied, "yes," he answered, "Talk it over with your wife and meet me here at one o'clock. You can tell me then. By the way, I want you in Mattawa first thing on Monday morning."

Heather was dealing out sandwiches to the kids like a croupier at a blackjack table when I arrived home with the news. Her answer came on the run as she ladled out the last bowlfuls of soup. "I think you should accept the offer, but we shouldn't sell our house." she said. "We may be back."

Little did we know at the time how accurate her foresight would turn out to be. The whole family loved living in the Soo, so it was not surprising when the kids, who were heavily involved with activities and friends, heard the news, they bolted for the door with screams of revolt.

The public school they attended was a five-minute walk from our house in a high-growth area of young families and was bursting at the seams. The schoolyard was overflowing with portable classrooms, so when Heather visited the school to tell them that we would be leaving, the principal, Mr. Upper, said to her with a smile, "We're going to miss your family, Mrs. Connelly. They are great kids. But I hope you don't mind if I do a cartwheel right here in the hall. And what kind of roses do you prefer, white or red?"

That Sunday night I was on my way in my company Volkswagen Beetle to Mattawa, a beautiful little town of about twenty-five hundred people situated southeast of North Bay on Highway 17. Anyone who has ever driven through the town is struck by its postcard charm, nestled as it is in a grove of huge white pine trees where the Mattawa River joins the mighty Ottawa River. The name, Mattawa, was given by First Nations people meaning "meeting of the waters."

I was filled with excitement over the opportunity and the many challenges ahead, and there were to be a few. Adding to the thrill of a new job was the realization that I was once again returning to my beloved Algonquin Park, where Weyerhaeuser had logging operations on a road leading into the community of Brent, located at Cedar Lake.

Fortunately, we were provided with a large company house on the main street of Mattawa at a nominal rent. This allowed us to rent out our home to a Weyerhaeuser forester who was being transferred from Mattawa to the Soo. Unfortunately, the company house was being renovated, so we could not move in immediately. In the meantime, we rented a twenty-two foot trailer in Turcotte's trailer park on the banks of the Mattawa River.

That experience could be the subject of a book all on its own, with three boys sleeping each night in our van and the baby occupying a slide-out linen drawer, which extended from beneath the master bed. It was early July and ideal on nice days when the kids were able to swim all day at the beach in front of the trailer and we could eat outside. Rainy days were from hell, at least that is how Heather described it when I arrived home each evening in time to light up the barbeque for supper. We reached a critical threshold within three weeks and decided to move into the house before the drywall was finished and the paint was dry.

Early on the first Monday morning of my new job, I was picked up at the Valois Motel by newly appointed general manager Karl Simmerling. Karl was oozing with enthusiasm and confident that with his new team we could bring the sinking ship into the harbour.

"Yes, sir, Brent, you have arrived in Mattawa at the right time," he said. "We are going to make this baby sing. Picture Weyerhaeuser Canada as a large wheel with Mattawa being the corporate hub and you, my friend, will be a vital gear in that hub."

Less than a year later, the last spoke had sprung and that old wheel had fallen off the wagon, left to rust in a ditch along the railway track just west of town. However, on that morning, I was as pumped as Karl by the time we reached the bush to meet the foremen and crews, which at that time totalled about sixty men.

That was the day I first met Clarence Clouthier. Clarence had been with the company for several years and had the position of logging superintendent. His Algonquin features and friendly personality reminded me of a younger "Hay Lake Joe" Lavalley—he was probably in his mid-thirties. As I came to know him better, I couldn't help but be impressed with his almost supernatural bush skills. To this day, anyone in Mattawa over the age of fifty can tell some pretty amazing tales about him.

Clarence was a genuine bushman who regarded a compass as a silly white man's trinket carried by feeble-minded timber cruisers and boy scouts with fuzzy cheeks. Like a Canada goose, his compass was built into his brain, and it never failed him. Stories were told to me of his many hunting and fishing exploits. It was said that there was never a moose or deer hunt that he returned from empty-handed—just the opposite.

One warm summer evening, Clarence and a few of his friends were hanging out on the downtown bridge over the Mattawa River. They were looking over the edge into the deep water and speculating about whether there were any giant sturgeon lurking on the bottom.

Clarence jumped into his truck and drove off, presumably to his home, and returned in a few minutes with a make-shift snorkel and cross bow. He dove into the river, like James Bond chasing an enemy submarine, and was out of sight for an uncomfortably long period of time, much to the concern of his anxious friends watching from the bridge. Eventually, he appeared sporting a huge grin and holding a rope tied around an expired forty-pound sturgeon. A round of applause broke out from the gallery of onlookers, which by that time included a number of townsfolk who were out for an evening stroll and had gathered to watch the underwater chase.

Apart from the harvest of fish and game—and logs—everything that Clarence Clouthier came across in the bush was of some value. In his spare time, he rounded up friends to pick pine and spruce cones for sale to tree nurseries.

He had a trapper's licence and harvested beaver, muskrat, and mink. Large yellow birch burls and other unusual tree disfigurements were collected to be used in the production of wooden bowls, ornaments, and coffee tables.

He organized high school students to pick princess pine for sale to the producers of funeral wreaths. (Princess pine is a variety of clubmoss sometimes referred to as ground fir or *Lycopodium obscurum*.)

As he walked the bush, Clarence was always on the lookout for white birch trees capable of providing bark for use in building birch-bark canoes. And to this day in Mattawa, there are many backyard patios that still display flat stones Clarence came across in the bush.

He was more than just a logger—he was a free spirit connected to the bush in ways that go beyond log trucks and bulldozers. He was like the deer and the moose. The bush was his home.

Many years after I had left Mattawa, I was saddened to hear that Clarence had been struck and killed by a falling tree as he drove his truck through an active logging operation he was supervising.

Three of my logging supervisors in Mattawa were connected to Clarence Clouthier in one way or another, and there may have been many more.

Timber cruiser Orval "Audie" Parent was Clarence's brother-in-law and was his passenger in the truck when he was killed. Fortunately, Audie was not seriously injured.

Logging foreman Jean-Paul Beaudoin and Clarence were long-time friends and had worked in the bush together for many years. One day in February, Jean-Paul came to me and said that he would like to take a few days off for a vacation. When I asked if he was taking a trip to a southern beach, he chuckled and explained in his charming French accent, "Not a chance. I never put my bathing suit on until Canada Day. This is a different kind of vacation. Each year around the first of March when there is a good crust, me and Clarence strap on the snowshoes and go to the bush to round up some beaver pelts—make more money in two weeks than we do logging for two months." Full details of that trapping junket were never known to me, nor was there any need for me to know.

Road construction foreman "Long Joe" Montreuil was another one of Clarence's brothers-in-law and, as the name would imply, was a tall, gaunt man who galloped through the bush with the strides of a charging moose.

Mattawa was more than just a place to work. It was also a good place to live, bringing with it some great memories and more stories. Our whole family became actively involved in the community, even though we lived there for less than a year. Everything we enjoyed in the city of Sault Ste. Marie was there, only on a smaller scale. And, yes, like most northern logging towns, there was some drinking. It's not that everyone in town drank; it's just that those who did were good at it.

I had been well warned about the custom of drinking on the job that the loggers maintained during the last afternoon before the Christmas break. Nobody before me had been able to do anything about the problem. It just happened year after year, as regular as turkey and mashed potatoes. Well, I was determined to break the pattern. It wasn't going to happen on my watch. Not a chance!

I started putting the word out at Thanksgiving that anybody caught drinking on the job on the last day of work before Christmas would be fired before Santa Claus had a chance to get his suit out of the closet and hitch up the reindeer. And there would be no second chances. Memos were circulated, and the subject was on the agenda of all our production meetings. Finally, the day arrived, and I was in my truck at the crack of dawn. I would visit every work site. Had to get into the spirit of the season and pass on greetings to my new crew. But, most importantly, I had to monitor the booze situation.

Everywhere I went that morning, I could hear the scream of chainsaws and the roar of skidders and bulldozers. Logs were flying out to the roadside landings and sawdust was piling up in heaps. It was like any other workday. I ate my lunch around a big fire with some of the men. We talked about where we would be logging after the holidays, and there wasn't even a hint of any drinking. Not even a mention. By one o'clock, I was feeling pretty good about the situation. My aggressive campaign had obviously brought results. So I decided to return to the office. Maybe it would be possible to go home a little early that afternoon to be with my family.

I cleaned up a couple of things in the office and jumped into my truck to go home, but decided instead to drive up to the garage to see if the crew buses had arrived back from the bush. They weren't there yet. Nothing in the parking lot except a few cars with women sitting behind the steering wheels. That in itself was unusual. I had never seen them before. Was I missing something?

The answer came in a minute or two, as the first of the three crew buses pulled into the yard. When the bus stopped, a swarm of giddy loggers cartwheeled out the door singing at the top of their voices, "We're here to log, not walk the dog." It was then that I knew why wives and girlfriends were sitting in the waiting cars. They had been down this road before. And now it was my turn.

I went over to greet the revellers and asked the first one I met, "Have you lads been drinking?"

"We haven't had a friggin' sniff of 'er, Brent," he slurred. "Christmas is for the kids. We do our drinking on New Year's Eve."

After I confirmed that the foremen who were driving the vehicles had not been drinking, I said to myself, "What the hell is the use?" So I jumped into my truck and stopped at the liquor store for a bottle of Little Brown Jug and went home to enjoy the Christmas celebrations with my family.

Christmas is the time for peace, and yes, there was peace in Mattawa for the next few days. That is, until New Year's Eve arrived. The kids had gone to bed early that night, and Heather and I were sitting quietly in front of the TV sipping a glass of wine while watching Guy Lombardo's band serenade in the New Year. As the countdown began in Times Square, we stood for a toast to each other. Then, the minute the ball descended at the stroke of midnight, the world ended and we found ourselves in the middle of World War III. Gunfire erupted all around us, as our wide-eyed kids came tumbling down the stairs. Mattawa was under attack from some kind of insurgency.

I ran out to the front step where I could hear an occasional shot in the distance, but couldn't see anything or anybody unusual. The shooting had subsided and, in a few minutes, everything was quiet again. It took a bag of cookies and a gallon of hot chocolate to get the kids back to bed, and our lives returned to normal.

A couple of days later I met Jean-Paul Beaudoin and asked him, "What the hell was that shooting all about on New Year's Eve?"

"*Tabernouche*," he said, "I should have warned you about that. There is a custom in Mattawa every New Year's. Some people take their rifles out to the backyard and fire a shot or two into the air at midnight. A few years ago, one guy was a little too tight, and while shooting into the air, mistakenly knocked a couple of bricks off the top of his neighbour's chimney. His neighbour was also out in his backyard, and when he saw his bricks flying apart in pieces, he decided to even things up by shooting a few bricks from the other fellow's chimney. By the time the dust settled and there were no more bullets, there was a pile of brick rubble in both backyards."

That story has triggered another one of my favourites, as told to me by Jean Paul . . .

Mattawa's social centre is the Legion Hall. And the town's Olympic sport is darts. Dart players take the game very seriously, and there are several organized leagues playing each night with a huge awards banquet held at the end of the season. The hall is divided into numbered courts, with the bartender serving as the custodian of fancy cases containing personalized darts. These cases are kept in a locked cupboard with the bartender having the only key. He also presides over the scheduling and designates which teams play in the individual courts. There is a time limit on each game.

The story is that a Mattawa resident once had a visitor from New York City. He was a big city fellow who was visiting Mattawa for the first time. One evening, his friend suggested that they go down to the Legion Hall for a friendly game of darts and a beer or two.

The Mattawa host picked up some spare darts from the bartender and arranged for the pair to play on Court 6. Their game was to begin at 8:00 p.m. after the completion of a league game on the same court. At five minutes to eight, the host said to his friend, "Drink up your beer, it's our turn soon."

At eight sharp, the other team was still playing and weren't showing any signs of winding up their game. The host approached one of the players, a big, burly guy with a scowl on his face. It looked like he was losing the game and was not in good humour.

"It's eight o'clock," the host told him, "it's our turn on the court."

"Bullshit to you," the big guy replied. "We're going to be finishing our game, and then you can play."

Then the trouble started. One thing led to another and the shouting began. In the meantime, the city fellow was checking out the exits, as he wondered, "What the hell am I in the middle of here? Is this the wild north that I have heard so many stories about?"

Soon to follow was the shoving. This was getting really serious, as the other dart games stopped and a crowd gathered. The obnoxious dart player took a poke at the host, who had two darts in his hand. Then, in a sudden fit of rage, he reared back and threw a dart at the big guy with all his might. It hit him in the leg and stuck there with only the feathers visible to the onlookers. The big guy fell to the floor, rolling and screaming, while clutching his injured leg.

The guy from New York was in a state of sheer panic, and thought, "This is a really bad situation. Are there any cops here in the Klondike? Will I ever see my dear wife and kids again?"

He just couldn't believe what happened next as the crowd broke out in a chorus of laughter. Up jumped the injured player, who limped over to beside the American and heaved the injured leg up onto a chair. Then with a grunt, he pulled the dart out of his leg, after which he rolled up his pant leg to expose, of all things, a beautifully hand-carved wooden leg.

And that was the day the poor fellow from New York City joined an exclusive club of previous newcomers to Mattawa who had also fallen victim to the old dart-in-the-wooden-leg trick.

As time went on, it seemed like we were beginning to turn Weyerhaeuser's operation around. But there were still many obstacles ahead. The forest had been mismanaged for many years with the best timber having been previously harvested to leave residual stands of very poor quality material (nothing new about that in those days). As a result, the American management was reluctant to invest in updating antiquated mill equipment and manufacturing processes. A troubled union management relationship, which had prevailed for a number of years, needed to be rectified, and the new team was beginning to make some improvements in that regard.

But it all ended one evening with a phone call. Our sawmill on the Big Jocko River was on fire (the same mill where Francis Conway worked as a saw filer). I jumped into my vehicle and drove up to have a look. The mill was located on the highway between North Bay and Temiscaming, and I could see the glow in the sky from several miles away. As I joined others gazing in disbelief and sadness at the burning ruins, I immediately realized that our Mattawa dream was drifting off with the smoke into the darkness of the cool night air. The mill was an important potential revenue stream, but we all knew that it would never be rebuilt.

A few weeks later after having disposed of mill log inventories, I was packing my bags for Sault Ste. Marie. Several months after that, the complete Mattawa operation was shut down permanently and Weyerhaeuser walked away forever. The Mattawa challenge cup was now history, lying in a ditch alongside that old corporate hub.

The decision not to sell our house in Sault Ste. Marie loomed tall as a good one. One day, I visited the school that the kids had formerly attended to advise the principal of their return. As I drove into the schoolyard, I could see that the portables had been breeding while we were away. There were many more than when we had left. As I walked down the hall, Mr. Upper came out of his office, and as soon as he saw me, his jaw dropped and the blood drained from his face. "Oh, my God," I could hear him think, "they're back!"

When I confirmed to him that the kids were indeed returning, he fainted onto the floor right there in front of me!

For the next four years, I worked for Weyerhaeuser at Sault Ste. Marie as logging superintendent and branch forester. However, cracks were starting to appear in the company's future in the Soo, translating into an uneasy feeling for many of the employees. It was becoming increasingly evident that logging operations in Lake Superior Park were about to be permanently terminated by the Ontario government in response to the pressure from environmentalists.

Algoma, Sault Ste. Marie, and Mattawa had been good to all of us, and so had the Weyerhaeuser Company, but now it was time to move on. Many friendships were left behind when, in 1975, I had the good fortune to be hired by the newly established Algonquin Forestry Authority and we packed our bags for the move back to Algonquin Park and to our new hometown of Pembroke.

PART III

# BACK HOME AND DOWN EAST

# Chapter 15: A Pass through Dunany

***"Oscar MacDougall could spin a yarn and knit you a pair of socks from the yarn in less time than it would take him to smoke a pipe-full of Quebec shag tobacco."***

—Emerson Noble, mechanic and WWII veteran, Lachute, Quebec

It seemed that many of the loggers working in Algoma Region had come from some other place. Locals jokingly referred to them as back-homers, down-homers, up-homers, or over-homers, in the case of immigrants. And, of course, these upstart migrants were never shy to boast that things were done better or quicker where they had come from.

It begged the question: if things were so good back home why, when living in Algoma, did they drone on so much about where they came from? It's because back home was where their hearts were. Back home was where they were nurtured by caring parents and spent their youth. It's where, as wide-eyed youngsters, they sat at the knees of weathered old-timers to listen to wonderfully enchanting stories about the good old days. Why would they not want to share some of that with others?

Many of the people I have talked about were from someplace else. Ben Harvey, Ab Hoffman, Scotty and Duncan Jamieson, Tony Vorlicek, and many others came to live and work in the highlands of Algoma. There was a good life there, in or near the comforts of a modern city like Sault Ste. Marie, with the added bonus of a wide variety of wilderness and outdoor pleasures within a few minutes' drive of home.

I, too, was a back-homer, and since I have pen in hand, I would like to seize the moment and pass on some memories and a few yarns about some down-home loggers, farmers, and the like, that I have known or heard of.

In today's world, the art of storytelling and the thrill of hearing stories has largely gone by the wayside in favour of Survivor and Google. Sadly, gone are the days when friends gathered around a cozy kitchen table with a pot of tea and a plate full of warm oatmeal cookies, sharing stories and hearty laughter. They talked and listened to each other. What more simple pleasure in life can there be than that?

Oscar MacDougall was one of my favourite storytellers. He lived on a farm in Dunany, Quebec, north of Lachute, and, along with his wife, Janet, were neighbours and good friends of my grandparents, Ida and Phineas MacVicar. Oscar was a part-time farmer but "worked out" (as they say when working away from the farm), mostly as a carpenter. Many cottages on the four lakes near his home still stand as testimony to his skill with a hammer and saw.

The community of Dunany can't be found on most Quebec maps. It's not a town, or a village, or even a hamlet. It has no lottery terminal, no gas station, no post office. It's simply a beautiful place, one that creates a serene feeling of peace for its grateful residents and summer visitors. It is their little slice of heaven nestled around four sparkling, spring-fed lakes (without the roar of motor boats) in the foothills of the Laurentian Mountains, the entrance to which is graced by a quaint, old Anglican church built close to a winding, former wagon road (now paved) at the bottom of a steep hill. It's here that the sweet sound of old-time hymns drift through open windows every Sunday evening in the summer.

One of the thrills of my youth was an evening visit to Oscar's with my parents and grandmother (Phineas had passed away before my birth). I would sit silently and spellbound with short legs dangling over the cover of the firewood box in the corner next to the wood stove. With every word, my imagination soared.

Upon entering the MacDougall kitchen, Oscar could barely be seen behind a cloud of dense blue smoke coming from a yellow-stemmed pipe, as he sat on a couch against a wainscotted wall behind the kitchen table. On the table was a package of Alouette pipe tobacco and a box of wooden matches—the ash tray was the nearby wood stove. Oscar's right thumb was yellow from lighting matches with the nail; the middle finger, black and calloused, from tamping live tobacco coals. His yellow teeth and wheezy laugh were signs of a lifetime of pipe-smoking, probably beginning when he was a young lad sitting in the shitter out behind the pig house.

St. Paul's Anglican Church, the gateway to Dunany.

When Oscar told his stories, he had a nickname for everybody. There was "Wee Willie" and "Big Arse Willie," "Hairy Pete" and "Baldheaded Pete," "Whispering Joe" and "Whistlin' Joe." My grandmother would jokingly remark, "I wonder what he calls us? Then maybe we don't really need to know."

There were some wild exaggerations, the kind that a young lad would never forget . . .

> I mind the time when we were thrashing oats at Phineas's place, when the old tomcat got tangled up in the thrashing machine. He came out of the chute like a cannonball, with four legs straight out, and soared over the henhouse like an eagle. And believe it or not, he staggered into the barn at milking time for his usual milk treat. Yes, siree, and that's as true as I'm sitting here.
>
> Did you ever hear about the time when Phineas's father was driving home from Lachute late one night with his mother in the cutter? The old lad was going down a hill too fast and the horse got away on him. The cutter upset in the ditch and threw Ma, ass over cream separator, head first into the snowbank. And that is why to this day that hill is called "Ma's Hill."

Oscar loved to fish and was often seen on one of the lakes or in the trout stream that ran by the front of his house. It amuses me to speculate on what his reaction would have been to the news that in the twenty-first century, our politically correct media and certain left-wing politicians insist on calling fishermen, fishers.

"What kind of bullshit nonsense is that?" he would snarl while clamping his teeth down on that old pipe. "A fisher is a furry, four-legged animal that slinks around in the bush. The next thing you know they'll be calling a lady deer hunter a huntess. Damn it all to hell, it's worse than a terror; it's a fright."

Oscar also worked as a local handyman and was relied on by many cottage-owners to build docks and do various repairs on their properties. Most of these people were wealthy residents of Montreal, about fifty miles from Dunany. He closed up their cottages in the fall and opened them up again before the owners returned in the spring. During the winter, he checked the snow build-up on cottage rooves and shovelled off the snow when necessary.

My father was in to visit Oscar one evening in late March. It was a cold night with still about two feet of snow remaining on the ground. They were enjoying a cup of tea when the phone rang.

"We all know how well-liked and charming Oscar was," my father said as he described what he overheard when Oscar answered the phone. "It was one of those nights that Oscar's charm was in full bloom," he added with a chuckle.

The call had come from a wealthy businessman from Montreal who had a large cottage on Clear Lake. He wanted his cottage opened up the last weekend in March. He was planning on entertaining some friends, while there was still ice on the lake and snow in the bush. They would like to do a little skiing, snowshoeing, and relaxing in front of the fireplace.

"Can you help me out, Oscar?" the old fellow asked as Oscar screwed up his face in agony. "And of course, I'd like you to pick up some groceries and liquor."

The request meant that Oscar would have to open up the road, shovel a bunch of snow, and carry in firewood. I could tell by his body language that he wasn't a bit thrilled by the prospect of it all. What nonsense. After all, the snow would all be gone in two or three weeks, making the job much easier. However, his unreceptive mood wasn't reflected in his response to the caller.

"It'll be my pleasure, Jimmie. We'll be thrilled to see you," he purred, all the time with a big scowl on his face when it should have been a smile. "You're as welcome as the flowers in May."

It wasn't until after Oscar had hung up the phone that Dad heard his true feelings on the matter.

"That stupid old son of a bitch," he growled. "I have more to do than to bull my way through the damn snow into his place, just so he can sit around the fireplace sipping on French cognac and puffing on big cigars. Why doesn't he go on a Caribbean cruise like the rest of his big-shot friends do this time of year?"

My favourite story told by Oscar was about another colourful Dunany character, Nelson Morrison, who, if there ever was a man deserving of a Kyoto carbon credit, it was him.

Nelson and Jessie Morrison and their five children were Oscar's other neighbours, just up the road on the way to the Dunany lakes. In between the two homes flowed a creek, which was the energy source for an old water-driven sawmill operated by Nelson. Above the mill, a timber-and-rock dam held back water that came from four lakes: Clear, Boyd, Black, and Curran. A large, wooden flume carried the water from the dam to the mill wheelhouse.

A smaller flume, which Nelson had built in 1925, tapped into the large one and ran water to a 110-volt DC generator, which for over twenty-five years produced electricity for lights in the home, sawmill, and horse barn. The barn was home to Nelson's old black horse, who will remain nameless for reasons that need not be explained.

Nelson Morrison's water-powered sawmill, Dunany, Quebec: "Bring on the rain, water is money."

In many ways, Nelson was a man ahead of his time. He was an inventor and shrewd entrepreneur, who was always looking for a better way of doing things. He was usually a quiet, soft-spoken man, except when a belt flew off a pulley in the sawmill. It was then that Phineas MacVicar could hear his roars while plowing in a field a half-mile away.

Nelson walked with a limp, a result of having broken an ankle in five places while working alone in the mill. That day, his screams of agony rising above the droning sound of the mill brought a frightened young son, Willis, and Oscar MacDougall to his aid. Young Willis was immediately dispatched to the house to fetch his mother and a bottle of rubbing alcohol.

I really don't know where to start in describing that old sawmill. It was through my boyhood friendship with Nelson and Jessie's youngest son, Ernest (or Ernie, as I called him), that I have been left with this wonderful image.

The mill had a circular head saw, edger, trim saw, slabsaw, and planer. Nelson always kept the saws sharp, and his lumber was well known for its excellent quality. There was no thick and thin lumber coming out the end of that mill—Nelson's two-by-fours were real two-by-fours, not the popsicle sticks they are today. However, the mill's efficiency and productivity were so dependant on water levels from the lakes that there were hot days in July and August when the mill could only operate in the mornings, or not at all. There had to be sufficient build-up of water in the mill pond above the dam.

But it was the sights, sounds, and smell of that old mill that has remained so clearly etched in my memory after all these years. The mill had a personality of its own—just like its captain. When there was a full head of water and the mill was operating full out, it shook and danced on its timber foundation, while the screaming saws sang, zinged, and whistled "pop goes the weasel" throughout the countryside. And it was a real treat to be inside the mill on a rainy day and hear rain pelting against the rumpled tin roof in rhythm with the whirling saws. It was like being on stage with Spike Jones.

On other days, when the water levels were lower, the shaking would be reduced to a mere quiver, the banging and clanging becoming nothing more than a murmur. It was then that Nelson could be seen holding onto the levers of the cable-driven log carriage as he attempted to saw a big pine or oak log, his tongue curling around outside a corner of his mouth as he coaxed a log through the saw.

And now to Oscar's story . . .

> It was a hot day one July when me, Phineas, Emerson Noble, and Dan Brown were loading lumber onto wagons from the end of Nelson's mill. The water was low, and Nelson was struggling with reduced power trying to saw some big, white pine logs. As he eased a log on the carriage through the head saw, the whole mill would slow down, until he reversed the carriage to let the mill's main flywheel regain its torque. Then it was another pass. It took him several tries to get a single board cut from the log.
>
> At one point, he was sawing a big, big, huge log, when all of a sudden, the banging and shaking stopped as the whole mill ground to a halt. Complete silence! The only thing we could hear was a volley of profanities coming from Nelson. His old dog, who was sleeping near a log pile, woke up and looked around, shaking his head in amazement at the stillness. The world had come to an end.
>
> We continued loading lumber with our heads down, quietly chuckling over Nelson's dilemma, when Dan offered an explanation, "Holy old jumpins, Nelson must have hit an awfully big knot."

In our modern world of Kyoto-mania and global-warming trauma, Nelson Morrison would have stood tall above the rest of us. Imagine a man making a good living operating a sawmill and producing his own electricity, while his neighbours read their Bibles with eyes squinting under the faint glow of coal-oil lamps.

And all this through the ingenious use of God's gift of water. There was no air or water pollution, only a little noise. And the only greenhouse gas that came from Nelson's operation was the gas that blew out the back end of that old no-name horse, as he puffed up the hill alongside the family home pulling a wagon load of slabwood to a cottage on Clear Lake.

But as in everybody's life, the old invariably makes way for the new. One of Nelson and Jessie's sons, Willis, wrote a marvellous history of his family, *From Horse and Buggy to Jet Age, A Story of the Morrison Family during the 1900s*. In the following excerpt, Willis describes an important transition in the lives of his parents:

> In the early 1950s, commercial power was brought into Dunany and then the commercial power lines were running past the Morrison house. The neighbours quickly got their houses wired and were soon lit up, but Nelson scornfully ignored all this stating that his power plant had been producing electricity for twenty-five years and he saw no reason to change.
>
> But he was ignoring a few things: first, the little power house was collapsing, the floor had caved in and Nelson had been forced to prop it up so that the generator would keep running. Also, the walls of the building were rotting and the flume leading into the little water wheel was constantly leaking.
>
> A secondary problem was that Nelson's plant produced direct current power which meant that about the only household appliance that Jessie could use was a clanking old washing machine with a direct current motor especially installed in it years before. The neighbours, however, with their newly acquired alternating current power, were enjoying the use of all kinds of gadgets and kitchen appliances, especially refrigerators. Jessie, glaring at the old icebox refrigerator in the corner of her kitchen, started to protest.
>
> Eventually it all came to a head when the next-door neighbour's house suddenly sprouted an impressive TV antenna on the roof. In the past, Nelson had always made occasional visits to MacDougall's to talk, but suddenly the visits increased and for longer duration.
>
> Jessie, left at home, soon realized what was happening and the domestic stress factor went up a notch or two. Finally in 1957, Nelson had the house completely re-wired and the commercial power hooked up. The old powerhouse was left to crumble after thirty years of use.

Across the gravel road from Nelson's sawmill was a hayfield that belonged to my grandparents. After Phineas's death in 1936, Ida continued to run the farm for a while with help from her two brothers, Johnnie and Hughie Martin. As a boy, I spent a lot of time around the farm in the summer. It was a hot ninety-degree afternoon in July, and I was helping Hughie and Ida take in hay. My grandmother was building the load on top of a wagon that was being pulled by a team of horses. Hughie and I were forking the hay up to her. (To maximize the load capacity, it was important to place the loose hay so that it formed square corners and not become cone-shaped in the middle of the wagon.)

It was one of those days that made a young lad yearn to jump into the cool waters of a nice lake. Yet here I was, working in a hayfield while my parents' cottage was only a mile over the hill on the shore of beautiful Clear Lake. But I had always been taught that for a boy to become a man, he had to learn how to work like a man. That is what I was trying to do until I saw Ernie Morrison come running across the field in my direction with a towel and a bathing suit wrapped around his neck. (The sawmill had shut down for the day at noon because of low water—Ernie was on the loose.) Old Hughie just looked up at Ernie with a quick glance and a twitch of his big black moustache and, without saying a word, handed him a spare pitchfork that he had brought along for such an occasion.

We both pitched hay for a while, but our motivation began to fade as the sun got hotter and our boyish giddiness began to set in. Hughie was watching us, but still didn't say a word as we went through the motions of working. Then it looked as if my prayers were going to be answered.

At the other end of the field, we saw another boy running in our direction. It was a city boy who was staying at one of the cottages on the lake. He was wearing a bathing suit and had come to get us to join him and the Rutherford girls for a swim. There were no more pitchforks, but Hughie didn't say anything as we continued to work while the city kid stroked the horses' manes and looked anxiously in the direction of the lake.

Just when I thought my friends were going to bail out on me and head for the lake, I saw my grandmother peek over the edge of the load and say something to Hughie. He put down his pitchfork, took an old red polka-dot handkerchief from his pocket to wipe a sweaty forehead, spit a deadly stream of snuff juice at a nearby grasshopper in flight, and said quietly while holding back a little smile on his big round face, "When you have one boy, you have one boy. When you have two boys, you have half a boy. But when you have three boys, you have no boys at all."

Then he leaned down and whispered to me, "Your grandmother thinks that you lads should go for a swim. Maybe that'll refresh you for a good day in the hayfield tomorrow. See you then, but don't bring your friends with you."

But before leaving Dunany, a brief tip of my hat to my grandparents, Phineas and Ida MacVicar. Their farm was homesteaded in 1836 by Phineas's Scottish forefathers. Four small fields, which had been cleared and picked over for rocks by three generations, perched on the side of a hill. The land supported a dozen dairy cows, a team of horses, and a handful of chickens and hogs. Not to mention a family of four. The balance of the farm consisted of about two hundred acres of mixed bush, which my grandfather logged very cautiously over the years. Another real example that farmers in those days had their crosscut saws hanging on the same wall as the horse's harness.

Farming wasn't easy in Dunany, and income was sparse. It came in small amounts from the sale of milk, eggs, butter, chickens, firewood, and maple syrup. Over a long winter, money from the sale of a gallon of syrup could make the difference between having or not having fresh oranges and a store-bought gift for their two young daughters at Christmas.

Proudly displayed on a rec-room wall in our home in Ottawa is a certificate. It is from the Canadian Red Cross Society, Quebec Provincial Branch, and designates Phineas MacVicar as the recipient. The certificate reads:

> The society acknowledges with gratitude your gift of maple products to the Duchess of Connaught Hospital at Clivden for the benefit of Canadian soldiers wounded in the European War of 1914–1915–1916–1917.

What more needs to be said about that unselfish couple, but God bless them both!

Five members of the original MacVicar generation are buried in a family cemetery in the corner of a field, a five-minute walk from the house. Graverobbers were a threat in the early 1900s as they sought fresh bodies for medical research and to steal valuables. It was common for families to bury their loved ones close by, and for a few nights after a burial, lanterns were maintained at the gravesite to deter would-be snatchers. The graves were marked only by upright fieldstones, as tombstones were an expensive luxury for frugal, hard-working farmers. Over the years, the cemetery became overgrown with bush and the stones began to lean. In the 1990s, the Noble and Connelly families installed a proper tombstone surrounded by a permanent wrought-iron fence. The cemetery continues to be maintained by the family to this day.

A visit to Dunany often includes a walk through dense bush to stand alone for a few minutes in the middle of that pretty little cemetery, now resting under the protection of a rich canopy of large hardwood trees. It is here that I am able to reach out and touch my past, and that is a very good feeling.

# Chapter 16: Farmers are Loggers, Too

***"The wood that I burn in my outdoor furnace is so green that I have to empty the water out of the ash pail every morning."***

—Truman Clark, farmer, Brownsburg-Chatham, Quebec

There always has been a special place in my heart for farmers. Maybe it's because farmers are so much like loggers. Often they are one in the same, as most farmers I know own their own bushlots out back some place, while many loggers were either raised on farms or are part-time farmers themselves.

Over the four decades that I worked in the forest industry, I have hired many people to work in the bush—foresters, timber cruisers, log scalers, forest technicians, and truck drivers, to mention a few. Not once in all those years was I ever disappointed in the outcome after having hired a person who had been raised on a farm. Not one time! The reason: I have yet to meet a farmer who couldn't get along with a neighbour or who didn't have a good attitude and work ethic. From there it came down to the experience and skills required.

Farmers possess a certain courage and grit. They face enormous risks as presented by wild swings in the weather and the marketplace and often-times a frightening financial burden resulting from necessary capital investments. Somehow, they always seem to find a way to overcome it all and carry on. Perhaps it is their great love for the land and their strong faith in God that gets them up at 5 o'clock in the morning with smiles on their faces.

Mark Anderson is an accomplished feature columnist for the *Ottawa Citizen* and a journalism professor at the Woodroffe campus of Algonquin College in Ottawa. He hits the nail on the head with an article he wrote on the subject of mandatory retirement at age sixty-five: "If you spent your entire working life on a farm, you don't stop tilling the fields or milking the cows on your 65th birthday for the simple reason that farming is not merely what you do—it's who you are."

Like loggers, farmers work under the faithful wing of Mother Nature. They have to. The last thing farmers do before going to bed at night is check the night skies for signs of weather for the next day. Is there a pink sky or a ring around the moon, or does the Big Dipper look like it's turning into a big dripper?

A friend of ours, Nelda MacCosham from Pembroke, was raised on a farm and describes the rule of thumb that her father used: If there is dew on the grass at nightfall, then the next day will be a good day for haying—more or less, that is.

These important questions all have to be answered before a plan can be made for the following morning. And all before the head of the weary farmer hits the pillow for the first rest of a busy day. Or, maybe it was the second rest of the day. Many farm houses I have visited have a couch in the kitchen up against the wall behind the big harvest table. Here, if needed after lunch, he could stretch out, snuggled up against a purring old cat for a fifteen-minute power nap before heading back into the fields. It's more likely, though, that lunch would consist of gulping down a thermos of tea, a couple of roast-beef sandwiches, and a fresh tomato and cucumber picked from a backyard garden while perched on the seat of a moving tractor.

Davis MacVicar is a semi-retired farmer who still goes to the barn every day to help out his son, Mark, in a large dairy operation on the edge of Brownsburg, Quebec. Recently, Heather and I had the pleasure of sharing a cup of tea and some cake with Davis and his wife, Carol, in the kitchen of their Brownsburg home. Davis is a large, jovial man with a thundering laugh and a huge, gripping handshake that could make the mightiest wince and drop to their knees. We have been good friends since we were boys. But now he is an old-timer—just like me.

Most farmers I have known have been blessed with good humour and a knack for storytelling—qualities, I'm sure, as important to their survival as gentle rains and warm sunshine. Davis MacVicar is one of those farmers—a storyteller in a class by himself. On that day, the stories flew like chaff coming out of the chute of a grain harvester. For two solid hours, we laughed and laughed until the cows came home, so to speak.

When we got on the subject of Arnold Johnston and the farmers' code about a tractor or pickup truck being stuck in a mud-hole, Davis had this to offer:

"Brent, I once had a similar experience to tell you about. It's one with a bit of a twist to it.

"My neighbour, Allie Dixon, was having some mechanical problems with his tractor and, as a result, was a little behind with his fall plowing. So I decided to go over one day and give him a hand. I was plowing along a treeline between Allie's field and his neighbour, Lorne Clarke, when I noticed Lorne's tractor bogged down to the axles in his field. There was no sign of Lorne, so I stopped my tractor and hopped over the fence to have a look.

"There had been a wet spell a week before and the ground was a little spongy. It looked as if the tractor had been there for a day or two, but on that particular day, the sun was warm and there was a strong breeze. I could see that the mud around the rear wheels was starting to dry up a bit. Maybe it could be freed.

"I jumped up on to the seat and started the tractor with the push-button ignition switch. I eased out the clutch and the tractor moved a bit. After rocking it a couple of times, I got off the tractor and kicked some dry ground under the tire tracks. Success came on the next try, and I drove the tractor to some high ground about a hundred feet away from the mud-hole.

"And then the devil entered the picture and made me do a bad thing. I cut a branch from a nearby spruce tree and brushed away all signs of my footprints. It was as if a mighty sky hook had descended and popped Lorne's tractor right out of the grasp of that nasty old mud-hole.

"I laughed all the way home that afternoon and well into the night. At one point my puzzled wife, Carol, suggested that I might want to sleep on the couch. Of course, I couldn't tell her about Lorne getting his tractor stuck. That would be the betrayal of a friend.

"For the next couple of weeks, I didn't hear anything about the incident. I knew that Lorne had recovered his tractor because, occasionally, I saw him driving it on the highway up to Brownsburg. I even chatted briefly with him a few times when we met uptown. He didn't say anything about his tractor, nor could I ask him any questions. The weeks went by and still no reports. I was baffled. And then it all came to a head just before Christmas when I met Lorne at a church social.

"'Davis,' he whispered with his head down and eyes pointed to the floor, 'Allie told me that you were helping him with some plowing this fall. Was it you who yanked my tractor out of the mud?'

"'Nope, it wasn't me,' I said with a straight face while just about choking on the pickled beet that I was eating.

"Lorne went on to explain that he and his son, Brian, went out to the field one night under the cover of darkness to pull out the tractor with their other tractor. They were shocked to see that it had been moved. And upon closer examination the next day, he couldn't find any sign of anybody having been there. No tractor tracks. No footprints. Nothing.

"'I haven't slept a wink all fall,' he groaned, 'trying to figure out what happened.'

"'Maybe it was divine intervention, Lorne,' I suggested with a slight grin as I looked around the hall at the huge crowd of our mutual friends and neighbours. 'But you'll have to make sure that nobody hears about this, Lorne. If they do, you'll never live it down. Rest assured that I won't utter a peep to anybody.'

"And I didn't say anything . . . at least not until after I had finished swallowing my egg-salad sangwich."

Now I can't say for sure if Davis added a "g" to his sandwich or not when telling me the story. But many of the folks back home do. Others replace a "v" with a "b," making culvert "culbert," and include an "l" to make "chimnely." They are all the same people who roar with laughter because I can't get rid of the "r"' in "warsh" or "fruneral." I have been trying for years but nothing seems to work—so now I say to 'ell with it.

Now, we're back to that hill of potatoes again. Whenever there is a connection between pickled beets and church, I break up over a story that involved my other grandmother, Annie Connelly, and my grandfather, Johnnie. They belonged to a Presbyterian church in Brownsburg and found themselves inviting a guest minister back to their home for lunch after a Sunday morning service. The minister's name was Reverend Pickle.

Annie had an elaborate lunch prepared. There was cold turkey, a variety of salads, homemade bread and a dish of her renowned pickled beets (the kind made with cloves).

Annie was a little uneasy about having a stranger as a guest for lunch, and to make matters worse, the minister was a bit on the pompous side. She hoped, however, to pull it off without incident and things started off well. At one point, while they ate, there was a lull in the conversation. It was then that Annie nervously picked up the bowl of pickled beets and passed them to the good reverend, saying, "Have a pickle, Mr. Beet."

One of the joys of my boyhood was the many opportunities I had over the years, especially when there was a crowd, to tease my grandmother about the day she served pickles to Mr. Pickle.

Another one of Davis' stories was about Dr. Mason, a beloved country doctor in the Brownsburg and Lachute area. He was well-known for his willingness to visit the sick or injured in their homes, and not pressing for payment for his services from people who he knew didn't have much money. But he had much less patience with people who did. After all, he had supplies and drugs to pay for, as well as his own household expenses. Sometimes, a bag of potatoes or a couple of chickens was just not good enough.

There is a story of a young logger who had been injured in an accident in the bush and came to see Dr. Mason in his office. He had three broken ribs and was in a lot of pain. In those days, the patient was taped up tightly several times around the upper body and then sent home and told to stay quiet until the ribs healed. In this case, Dr. Mason knew that the logger had worked that winter in the shanties and would have come out in the spring with a few dollars in his packsack.

"That will be two dollars," Dr. Mason told the young logger as he put away his roll of tape.

"I don't have any money, Doc. Lost it all in a poker game last Saturday night," the logger replied.

"Well, then, give me back my damn tape," growled Dr. Mason.

The report of what happened next came from an old fellow who overheard all of this while sitting in the waiting room. "Dr. Mason grabbed hold of one end of the tape and started ripping 'er off. The young lad was hollering like a stuck pig as Doc spun him around like a top. Prit' near screw-nailed the young bugger into the floor."

There is another story about Dr. Mason and a large farming family from Shrewsbury, a small community a few miles north of Dunany. Three of the older boys had returned home from a logging camp where they had worked for the winter. Shortly afterwards the youngest came down with scarlet fever, and Dr. Mason was summoned. He immediately placed the family under quarantine and advised that no one was to leave the home until they were told to do so by him.

Over the next two or three weeks, he made the long trip from Lachute to the farm several times to check up on his patient. One day, after having been to Shrewsbury the day before, he was in the post office in Lachute and met a fellow he knew from Dunany.

"You know, Doc," he said, "I think that you're going to have trouble collecting for all your trips to Shrewsbury. I know that bunch, and they're a shifty lot."

"Don't worry, I'll take care of it," Dr. Mason replied quietly.

On the next visit, Dr. Mason found his patient fully recovered, and with the whole family gathered in the kitchen, he placed his little black bag up onto the kitchen table.

"Now," he began, as he pulled a pump spray-can out of the bag, "I'm going to have to spray the inside of your house to disinfect it to protect your neighbours. But the biggest problem of all is that this dreadful disease is spread mostly by people passing money from one to another. That's how serious epidemics start. So fetch all the money you have in the house and put it right here on the table, so I can spray that, too."

Immediately, the young lads scrambled up the stairs to the bedroom loft and, in a few minutes, came down with their bankrolls earned from a long winter of logging. Dr. Mason sprayed the bills, one by one, giving him the opportunity to count the bounty at the same time. When he finished, he slipped the amount to cover his bill in to his little black bag.

"There you are, boys," he said. "That will save you a trip out to my office in Lachute to pay the bill. Now you're paid up in full."

Just up the road from where the loggers lived was another farm that also supported a large family, including three young and very attractive girls in their late teens. Some of the farm lads around Lachute had heard of the girls, and one Saturday night, decided to drive back and introduce themselves and share their charms.

Four of them piled into an old Model A Ford and started up the road to Shrewsbury. It wasn't very long before they made their first mistake of the evening. They stopped in at the Laurentian Hotel in Lachute and purchased a supply of beer. Their second mistake was a Dunany pit stop in a roadside gravel pit. It seemed that the time just flew by as one dead soldier followed another.

It was late by the time they reached the farmhouse. All the lights were out, and the girls were in bed. Even the old watchdog didn't wake up as the car did a figure-eight U-turn in the front yard. Nothing to do now but head back to Lachute!

One of the lads was flaked out in the back seat when the old car started down the big hill at Black Creek. Half way down the hill, the brakes gave out and, as the blurry-eyed driver struggled to maintain control, the others started to shout. This wakened the back-seat passenger, who jumped up to get a quick glimpse of the narrow little wooden bridge, looming quickly before them at the bottom of the hill.

"Double-clutch her and throw her into reverse," he screamed at the top of his lungs.

Despite everything, reports are that they made it without incident.

One of Shrewsbury's long-time residents was known far and wide throughout the Lower Ottawa Valley and Laurentian foothills. He was a mountain man who dabbled in a little farming, logging, trapping, and just about anything else that would turn a dollar. However, it was bear hunting that he was known for mostly. Locals called him the "bearman."

He hunted black bears throughout the countryside and sold the furs to a fellow from Montreal, who resold them to rich Americans for fireplace and trophy-room adornment. The furs had to be of high quality, but sometimes the bearman took the odd shortcut.

One summer, he shot a ratty-looking, near-death bear whose fur was a spotty mix of black and grey. The bearman brewed up some kind of restoration concoction and took great pains to comb the potion through the fur. By the time he finished, the bear's fur had a shiny gleam to it. Looked good enough to be worn by a foot soldier in front of Buckingham Palace. He sold the fur to the broker for the usual price, and that was the end of that, until a month or so later when the two met once again.

"You know that fur you sold to me last month?" the broker said. "Well, it was good for nothing. Couldn't give the damn thing away. It's still sitting out in my garage, and the squirrels are starting to eye it up for their winter nest."

"Don't know what you're doing wrong," the bearman replied. "It sold awfully well when I had it."

Davis had his own bush on the farm and also did a little logging with others. He tells of one late winter afternoon when he, Nelson Tomalty, and Billy O'Brien were driving out of the bush on the east road "inbacka" Dalesville. Nelson was driving his own pickup, and John Fox was behind them somewhere coming out with a truck-load of logs:

> Nelson was driving a little too fast as we came down a steep hill with a sharp corner at the bottom. As we turned the corner, the right front wheel bit into the snowbank and the truck began to swing crossways on the road.
>
> "Hang on boys," Nelson shouted. "I think we're going to change ends."
>
> As the rear end of the truck swung around to the opposite snowbank, over she went. Laid that puppy right on her side. There we were, the three of us scrambling out of the one upright door. We were like three cats trying to escape from a potato sack.
>
> The road was blocked, tools were spilled all over the road, and a chainsaw had been pitched up on top of a snowbank. Things were looking pretty grim, and to make matters worse, John Fox was behind us with a loaded log truck. Would he see us from the top of the hill and be able to stop before piling into the upset truck? We had to act fast. What to do?
>
> After looking around for a minute, we decided that we might be able to spring-pole the truck back onto its feet. So Nelson grabbed the chainsaw and cut a maple sapling about sixteen feet long and four inches at the butt. We chained the pole vertically to the frame of the truck (the large end of the pole was attached to the frame at ground level where the truck rested, the other end on the upper side).
>
> Then the three of us pulled down on the top end of the pole and let it go, trying to spring the truck back onto its wheels. We could move it three or four feet, but not enough to flip it back on its wheels. Finally, Billy volunteered to shinny up to the springy end of the pole. That would give us more lift.
>
> With Billy hanging on for dear life, Nelson and I pulled the small end of the pole down to within a couple of feet from the ground. That's when the roaring started, as Billy sailed up into the air when we let the pole go. Just about catapulted him over the

hill into downtown Brownsburg. Two or three more tries failed, but we were getting closer each time Billy took flight.

In a few minutes, John Fox arrived and had no trouble stopping his truck. However, he wasn't any help to us for a few minutes, while he paused to recover from a laughing fit. Finally, with the help of John and another fellow who was with him, we were able to upright the truck and head for home.

(Nelson's bankshot reminds me of a former colleague of mine, Bob Coleman, operations supervisor with the Algonquin Forestry Authority, and his advice on winter driving in the bush: "Remember, for every mile of road, there are two miles of snowbank. So, aim 'er down the middle, lads.")

Davis goes on to describe another logging experience he once had . . .

Nelson, his young helper, and I were cutting four-foot pulpwood one day. It was just before noon when we cut a rotten old maple tree into four-foot lengths and found the tree to be hollow from its butt to the top. The cut-up tree was lying in front of our lunch place, and as we sat there toasting our sangwiches, we noticed a squirrel run into the hole in the butt of the first block. In a few seconds, he flew out of the other end. Then he ran quickly another foot or so on the ground and into the hole on the large end of the second block. Out he came again from the small end. This was repeated for another two blocks. The old bluegrass tune, "Fox on the Run," was now matched by "Squirrel on the Run." What was he doing? Probably just having a little fun running through a tunnel or looking for a mate.

By this time, we were standing up watching the amazing performance. When the little critter came to the last block, he didn't come out the other end. Maybe he had found what he was looking for. The curious young lad who was working with us grabbed a three-foot scale stick and went to the top end of the block. He poked the stick into the block, and suddenly the squirrel raced out and ran up the scale stick and up the arm of the startled youth. The squirrel paused on his shoulder long enough to brush a bushy tail across his face, after which he jumped onto the ground and disappeared up a tree. It took the shaken fellow about fifteen minutes to find the scale stick, which he had thrown into the bush at the frisky squirrel.

In the 1940s and 1950s, logging was widespread in the Laurentian foothills, and remote logging shanties were scattered throughout the area. After working hard from spring until fall in the fields, many farmers took their

Davis MacVicar, farmer, Brownsburg, Quebec: "Don't need a come-a-long or a bumper jack if you can make a good slingshot."

teams of horses into the bush to log for the winter. This was an important supplement to the usually meagre family income from cultivating a dirt farm laced with stones.

There is a story about a hard-nosed local lumberman who once paid a visit to one of his logging camps on a cold winter day. (Davis provides an example of his reputation for astuteness: when one of his men requested a week off to get married, he asked, "Why would you need a week? It only takes half an hour to get married.")

The lumberman spent most of his time around the sawmill and office in town, so for the most part, the bush operation was left to the camp foreman to manage. When he arrived at the camp on this trip, the old fellow went in to see the clerk in the camp office. The camp foreman had also been called in from the bush for the visit. The purpose was to review the payroll and production records and to talk about the operations ahead.

After a few minutes of checking and with a worried look on his face, he said to the foreman, "We've got a problem here. You have thirty-five men working in the bush, and they are making fifteen dollars a month, plus board. You are making twenty dollars a month, plus your board, and the damn cook is making the same as you. We can't have that."

"That's easy to fix," smiled the foreman. "Just give me another five dollars a month and I won't say anything to the cook."

"Not a chance," yelled the old fellow. "You go into the cookery right now and tell the cook that his wages are being cut to eighteen dollars a month starting today."

"I can't do that," complained the foreman. "The men will be in for supper in a couple of hours. The cook will quit when he hears this news and then where will we be? And what about breakfast tomorrow morning? I can't cook. Can you?"

"Just do it," instructed the old lumberman. "He won't quit. Where is he going to go from away back here in the middle of the bush on a twenty-below zero night?"

The foreman went into the cookery and gave the cook the bad news. Without hesitation, he ripped off his apron and slammed a big meat cleaver down onto the chopping block he was working on.

"I quit," he screamed as he went into the back room to get his packsack, then stormed out of the cookery and started walking down the long road to town with his back facing the setting sun.

Within minutes, the clerk, foreman, and their head-office visitor had gathered in the cookery to figure out what to do next. The meat was already cooking in the oven and pies were on the sideboard. All they would have to do was peel the potatoes and prepare a few vegetables.

The men had arrived in from the bush, and just as the potatoes were beginning to boil, there was a gentle knock on the cookery door. It was the cook. "Can I have my job back?" he asked the foreman shyly. "I met one of the teamsters down by the stable, and he told me that I had a two-day walk ahead of me to get to Lachute. On second thought, maybe I'll stay for the run. But I sure as hell won't be back next year. It's the first time ever that I made more money at the beginning of a job than at the end. Sounds upside down to me."

Talking about teamsters, logging was brisk in the same camp during the war years. The logging area was under the pathway of RCAF training aircraft, and planes commonly flew over the operation. One day a teamster was hauling a sleighload of logs across an ice road on Lake Louisa. There had been a January thaw and there was some slush on the surface of the lake. It was not a good day for the sleigh haul.

As the hard-working teamster struggled to coax his team across the lake with its heavy load, a plane appeared over a hill flying at an abnormally low level. When the pilot saw the sleigh below him, he decided to have a little fun. He banked around at the end of the lake and came back a few feet above the surface of the lake and buzzed the sleigh. The horses reared up, and it took all the teamster's strength to control them as he sat on a "dry arse" up on top of his load.

(A "dry arse" is a potato sack filled with dry straw which the teamster sat on to keep his rear end dry.)

"That was fun," thought the idiot pilot. "Why not try it again?"

Once again the plane buzzed the frightened animals. The horses reared up for the second time. This time, in anticipation of the attack, the teamster was down on the ice walking alongside the sleigh. As he fought to reign in the excited team, he fell face-down into the slush. Finally, after stumbling up onto his feet, he managed to get his team settled down.

But the fun was over for the pilot. He was flying too low as he banked away from the lake, and the tip of a wing caught the snowbank at the lakeshore. Down he went as the plane landed and flipped over on the ice. He was unhurt from the crash, but the plane was badly damaged. Only the exhausted horses can tell us what transpired when the angry teamster arrived on the scene of the accident.

A footnote to this story: the next night, two military officials showed up at the camp looking for somebody to pull the wrecked plane out to a public road. The eager volunteer was the same teamster who had been buzzed by the plane. He told the men in the camp afterwards that, as soon as he hooked his team up to the plane, they started to run like he had never seen them run before. He couldn't hold them back, so he just let them go. By the time they reached the road, broken pieces of the plane were scattered all over the bush and the horses were pulling nothing but a bare chain with what remained of the pilot's cockpit seat dangling from the end and bouncing off trees.

It wasn't long after the visit with Davis that I dropped into a farmers' display while attending the International Plowing Match near Keene, Ontario. I was given a large yellow lapel button stating "farmers feed cities." From time to time, on a Sunday afternoon when we are taking a leisurely stroll through Ottawa's downtown Byward Market, I wear the button as a show of respect and as a reminder to the city folk of the important role that farmers play in the good life we all enjoy. Usually, when passers-by see the button, they make eye contact with me and smile. Because they're the ones who know that most things they pick up in a Loblaws store have a farmer's hard work stamped all over it. And maybe when that same farmer has done a little logging along the way, they may even find a trace of him in a Rona store.

# Chapter 17: The Chainsaw Man

*"You don't need a pickup truck to drive into the bush when you can ride to work on one of Colin's chainsaws."*

—Old-time Manitoulin Island logger

The first chainsaws were beginning to make an appearance in the late 1940s. First came the awkward and very heavy two-man saw. Next was a bulky one-man saw—a little lighter, but still a man-killer to operate. As one logger described his first use of a chainsaw, "It was supposed to be a one-man saw, but it was so heavy that it took two of us to carry it around in the bush. And we had to hire a couple of squirrels to pick up the nuts and bolts that were flying off it."

Back home, Colin McOuat is a legend in the chainsaw business. He is the kind of man that books are written about. Since I hope somebody will do that some day, I won't steal the thunder from a possible biography. Instead, just a brief rumbling.

Colin's career was dedicated to a family-owned business founded by his father in 1936, the Farmers Supply Company of Lachute (more recently forming part of the McOuat Group of companies.) Initially, the company was the eastern Canadian distributor of Pioneer chainsaws. Later came the Canadian distribution of Jonsered and Husqvarna chainsaws. Safe to say that Colin and the boys have been sawing it off for over fifty years, and are still at it.

There was much more to Farmers Supply Company than chainsaws. Every farmer's need was met from fence staples and tractors, to milking machines and walk-in coolers. There were also some interesting deviations into the restoration and resale of Beaver aircraft, sales of outboard motors, and the importation of Honda cars. The company had an entrepreneurial spirit of adventure and discovery.

Perhaps what has intrigued me the most, however, was their brave entry into the snowmobile business in the 1960s, namely through the introduction of the Hus-Ski Snow Traveller. Colin McOuat was personally involved in the design, testing, and sales of that revolutionary machine. His friendly face breaks out into a broad smile when talking about that venture.

Many old-time loggers and trappers are familiar with the Hus-Ski, as are members of numerous spirited families of the time who used them for their own fun-in-the-snow outings. Unlike the modern single-unit construction of modern snowmachines, the Hus-Ski consisted of two parts: the front comprised the drive section with engine, dozer-type tracks, and a wraparound handle bar with controls, while a tow bar and pin connected the drive section to the passenger's sled. (The machine incorporated a work-horse "pull" engineering principle instead of the "push" design of today's high-speed machines.)

Recently, I visited Colin in his modern Lachute office, which looks more like a museum than any office I have ever seen. Admission could be charged to browse through this wonderful step-back-in-history display. The orderly presentation includes a large model of a Beaver airplane hanging from the ceiling, various outboard motors, a cream separator, antique kitchen ranges, and even some seats from the old Montreal Forum.

But what stopped me in my tracks was a full-scale prototype of a Hus-Ski snowmachine, powered by a chainsaw. It was designed for use by loggers, prospectors, and trappers who worked in remote locations. (Not a practical concept on modern operations where loggers are now able to drive their pickups to within a stone's throw of the stump.)

In today's world of sophisticated, high-speed mass transit, commuters ride to work in bullet trains, GO trains, and O trains. I am amused by an imaginary account of a day in the life of a logger, who may have used a Hus-Ski snowmachine to drive to work many years ago . . .

After breakfast, the chainsaw was retrieved from under the bunk bed, where it had been put to keep warm on a forty-below night. The Hus-Ski was parked near the front door of the shanty, where the logger loaded up the

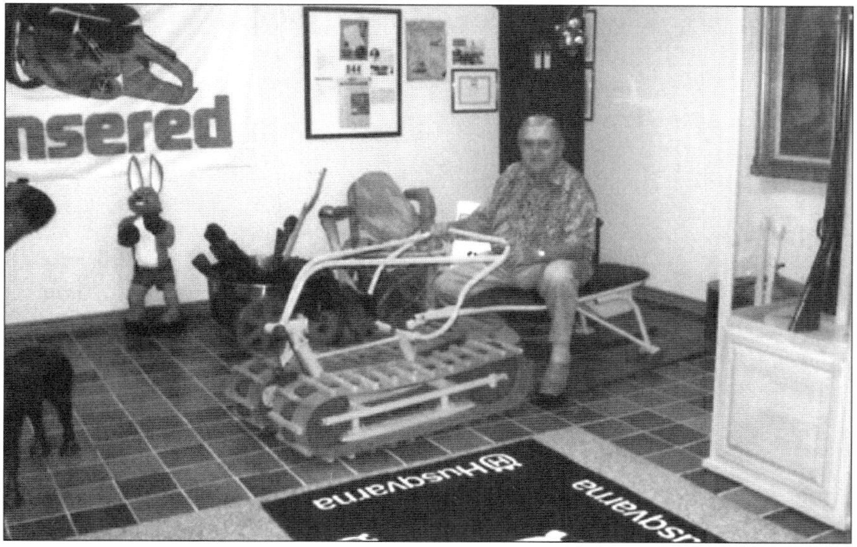


Colin McOuat, the chainsaw man, astride his beloved Hus-Ski Snow traveller in his office/museum, Lachute, Quebec.

storage compartment under the cushioned seat of the sled. The cargo consisted of a supply of gas and oil, a pair of snowshoes, and a packsack containing a double lunch.

Before boarding the sled, the logger used a small wrench to remove the chain and bar from the saw. The saw was then clamped onto the front section of the machine, and the chain was connected to the drive sprockets of the saw and tracks. Then the logger boarded the sled, gave a pull on the chainsaw starter cord, and took off like a scalded dog.

Upon arriving at the logging site, the chain and bar were reinstalled, and the logger used the saw to fell trees all day. At quitting time, the saw was reattached to the snowmachine for the trip back to camp.

Sounds far-fetched? Maybe a little. But that was the concept, and for another era, it was an idea that had to come.

And that about sums up Colin McOuat, a man who is always looking down the road for a new concept to explore.

# Chapter 18: A Maritime Logging Story . . . Wha?

***"When you meet Newfoundlanders, they are either on the way home, or planning to go home, or talking about their last trip home."***

—Anonymous mainland Canadian, Marine Museum, Winterton, Newfoundland

Loggers are loggers and back-homers are back-homers, whether they work in Algonquin Park, Lake Superior Park, Inbacka Mattawa, or Down East. Nothing really changes, except maybe the language, and that is why I love to travel to our Maritime provinces. It is there that I seek out opportunities to chat with locals for the sheer enjoyment of hearing them tell tales, seasoned with their wonderful dialects. It's sweet music for me . . . wha?

A few years ago, we were boarding a ferry in Port-aux-Basques, Newfoundland, on a very rainy and cold evening. As we waited in the parking lot, we noticed a buddy standing off to the side, dressed in a full-length yellow slicker. He smiled at me and said what sounded like, "Witwaw."

"What in hell did he say?" I asked Heather. She was as puzzled as I was. The only way I was going to find out was to have a conversation with him.

The answer came right away. "Yes, me son, it has been raining for four solid days. She's plenty wet . . . wha?"

What classic stuff . . . wha?

Another time we were camped on the Exploits River in Newfoundland and took an early morning walk down to the public dock. A buddy came along in an old pickup truck with a chainsaw and some skidder cable rattling around in the back. The truck had bald tires and three fenders flapping—the fourth was missing. I could tell he was a logger. But today he was a fisherman. He was checking to see if the salmon were running yet, and after spotting us, came over for a chat.

"I thinks you're not from around here, wha?"

I told him he was right and that we were from Ontario.

Then he went on to explain. "That mainland ain't for me. Me and the wife were up your way last summer when we took a drive out to Alberta to see some buddies. On the way back we were supposed to get on a bridge in

Montreal, but gots all tangled up in a damn tunnel near Montreal. You know the tunnel that goes underneath that big son of a bitch of a river you gots up there. What's the name of that big river, wha?"

"That's the St. Lawrence River you're talking about," I said.

"Yeah, yeah, dat's 'er, alright," he replied. (And there we were, a stone's throw from the Gulf of St. Lawrence.)

Before one of our trips to Newfoundland, Heather read in a magazine that the best fish and chip restaurant in Canada was in St. John's. It was called Chess' Fish and Chips and was located near the harbour. So a visit to Chess' was included on the itinerary. As we approached the restaurant, we could see a couple of seamen sitting on the curb eating a feast of golden fish and chips on a paper plate. Above them and flush against the wall was a small Pepsi sign with the name Chess'. There was no fancy overhanging sign or canopy, just the simple Pepsi sign.

Inside the open door were four or five booths and a row of stools surrounding a counter. It was a beehive of activity. Every booth was full, and through an opening into the kitchen, we could see four or five buddies scurrying around frying fish in a cloud of smoke. We found a couple of stools next to four seamen who were laughing and chatting while enjoying their lunch, and gave our order to a very busy waitress.

It was our first day in St. John's, and we were still trying to find our way around the city. Heather was looking for a mall to buy some designer rubber boots and asked the waitress for directions. She was delivering an order and said that she would be right back to help us out. In the meantime, one of the men in the nearby booth overheard this and quickly approached Heather with a great big Newfie smile.

"I hears that you wants to find a maaall, lady," he said. "Well, we gots the biggest maaall east of Toronto right here in St. John's. She's a three-storey beauty with a couple hundred stores, and she ain't far from here."

Then he turned to me and told me to come outside with him so he could give me directions. He pointed up a hill to a stoplight and said, "She's some simple, mate. Only one turn. Just goes to the top of the hill and turn left at the light. It's out the highway straight ahead about three miles on your starboard side."

I thanked him, and he went back to join his friends.

When we finished the delicious meal, we walked out to the car and I drove up to the light as instructed. I turned left and drove, and drove some more, for about ten miles. No mall in sight. Nothing but bush. I thought I was back at Mile 100. Finally, the highway went through a huge black spruce swamp, at which point I turned around and headed back into the city. We didn't see any wild geese along the way, but we should have.

Can you imagine the fun that bugger had when he went back to the booth to tell his friends all about it?

"Yes, sir, mates. Them friggin' mainlanders will gets a good tour of the island this afternoon. We may have to throws them a line."

But that's not the end of it for any Newfoundlanders tuned in to this. Because the next time I bump into a Newfoundlander who is looking for the tunnel that runs under that big son-of-a-bitch of a river in Montreal, he had better pack a double lunch and be prepared to be away from the Rock for a while. And dat's for sure, bye!

Terry Noble is a good friend of mine, as well as my first cousin. He, too, is a UNB graduate forester and currently works for Frasers Paper Inc. in Edmundston, New Brunswick. He is responsible for the supply of raw material to various forest products manufacturing facilities in that province.

There is a long-standing custom in the logging business: when the season comes to an end during spring break-up, loggers often get together for a close-out party. Terry tells of the time when he was a supervisor in a logging camp in northern New Brunswick, which had closed down for the break-up, and he and his colleagues decided to go out on the town in keeping with the tradition. The plan was to go for dinner at a roadhouse well-known for its exotic stage entertainment.

One member of the group, an old road foreman, declined to go along. He felt that his wife wouldn't approve of him casting lustful eyes on a bevy of strippers. Anxious to include him, Terry and his friends apparently stretched the truth a bit and convinced the old fellow that the establishment was under new management.

It now had a family venue and that if there were to be any girls appearing on stage, they would be singing good old-fashioned songs along with a karaoke machine. In light of this new information, the old logger agreed to join the group.

Everyone enjoyed their dinner, after which the stage lights came on and a scantily clad stripper appeared from behind a curtain. She went into her dance routine and threw a few items of clothing onto the loggers' table, which was close by.

After a few minutes, the old road foreman leaned over to Terry and with a big grin, drawled, "I don't think she's going to sing 'Rock of Ages'. . . wha!" (Terry adds that the old-timer didn't look towards the exit once and stayed to enjoy the balance of the evening with his friends.)

Maritimers are a warm and generous people. A fun-loving Newfoundlander may send you on a wild-goose chase from time to time to keep you alert, and remind you that mainlanders are just plain dumb, but that same person would give you the slicker off his back to keep you dry.

# Chapter 19: Oh, My Goodness Gracious

***"I'm eighty-nine years old and weigh eighty-nine pounds. Now to check my weight I don't need my bathroom scales anymore—just a calendar on the wall."***

—Kathleen (Auntie Kay) Noble, everybody's favourite aunt, Lachute, Quebec

Loggers are constantly struggling with equipment breakdowns, market slides, and the challenges of bad weather. So it is little wonder that they commonly use profanity in a most descriptive and sometimes poetic manner. At least some of them do.

And when was the last time any of us heard Johnnie Shaw blurt out, "Oh, my goodness gracious, I wish that nasty rain would stop soon"? Or Scotty Jamieson explode with, "Aye, my good heavens, but that stubborn little mud-hole sure took a long time to heal up"?

Instead, the commentary would more likely start with a son-of-a-bitch and end with a son of a whore, with lots of other stuff in between.

So it was with a little nervousness that I included some moderate profanity in my first book, *Holy Old Whistlin'*. I fully expected it would cause some flashback and that I would hear from a disgruntled reader or two. But I didn't. Not one peep.

There was one incident, however, that nicked on the subject and I would like to share that.

One of life's treasures that most of us have enjoyed is a loving aunt. I have been lucky to have had several. One of them is Kathleen (Kay) Noble of Lachute, Quebec. My sister, Janice, and I have been calling her Auntie Kay since we were little kids, and still do, as she charges full blast into her ninetieth year. Our families also call her Auntie Kay, as do most of the residents of Dunany and Lachute where she now lives in a seniors' apartment.

She is not very big in stature and is a little more canted than she once was when she stood straight and tall as a younger woman. But she is mighty in spirit, determination, and her zest for life—a genuine octogenarian dynamo. So, if there ever was one who could make good use of a telephone-answering service, it is Kay. She is rarely at home, instead pointing her little Toyota Tercel from one church supper or bazaar to another. A couple of years ago, she stopped playing in a ten-pin bowling league on Wednesday nights—the explanation being that regular Monday night carpet bowling outings at her church provided enough exercise.

She drives to her cottage on Clear Lake, about fifteen minutes from Lachute, where she still spends most of her summers, providing her neighbours are around for company. However, a few years ago, the word spread throughout Lachute that Kay had been pulled over on the Dunany Road by the Sûreté and fined seventy-nine dollars for speeding.

When I heard the rumour, I gingerly asked her about it. With a little smile that she tried hard to hide by turning her head away, she coyly replied, "Those darn cops have little to do but to pull over a little old lady going to church. They should be out catching robbers."

I have my own theories about the incident. I have never known her to drive more than sixty or seventy kilometres per hour, but having followed her a couple of times, was always amused in my inability to see her head over the headrest on the driver's seat. Could it be that a police officer caught up to her car as it drove down the winding road, apparently without a driver, and he pulled her over out of curiosity? It's not a stretch to expect that at that point he may have received an earful from the feisty driver and reciprocated with a fine. Although I can never resist the opportunity to tease her about the incident, her response is consistently the same. The truth will forever remain a mystery, at least for me.

Kathleen (Auntie Kay) Noble, Lachute, Quebec: "Always a smile—never a frown."

Kay is a remarkable woman in so many ways. Since she was a little girl growing up on the MacVicar farm in Dunany and walking two miles to school wearing moccasins and leggings on a thirty-below day, she has maintained a daily journal. It wasn't just a few words scratched on a calendar. It was a detailed account of the day's activity. The tradition was a family one, as her sister (my mother) and their mother did the same.

The recording of information didn't stop with a daily diary. To this day, Kay maintains a log book which is kept on the top of her freezer. It records every date that the freezer was defrosted, from the time it was first plugged in. Another log book records each time she cooked a turkey for a church supper over the last fifty years. Information includes the weight of the turkey, the price per pound and how many people attended the supper. Now how is that for keeping track of things?

Kay has one son, Terry, the karaoke man, who lives in Edmundston, New Brunswick. Terry does a wonderful job of caring for his mother and looking after her needs. However, because he lives so far away, Heather and I try to back him up where we can with visits and phone calls. It has been a long-standing custom for her to spend Christmas in our home. She is usually with us for three or four days and enjoys the company of our children and grandchildren.

In 2005, we picked her up a couple of days before Christmas, and since she loves to read, and Holy Old Whistlin' was just off the press, I gave her a copy. I teased her by pointing out that she might stumble on some bad words here and there. Over the next day or so, every time I looked at her, she had her nose in the book. And once in a while she would utter a quiet little giggle. When I asked her how she was enjoying the book, she would just simply say with that little crack of a smile mentioned earlier, "You sure worked with some interesting men."

On Christmas Day the family gathered at our home. Our daughter, Kathy, worked with a young fellow who was not able to be with his family, so we had invited him to join us. Dave was a personable young lad and quickly made himself at home. He joined right in with all the banter and fun. At one point, a few of us were sitting around chatting in the living room and the subject of *Holy Old Whistlin'* came up. Kay sat quietly at the end of a chesterfield taking it all in.

The question of the profanity was discussed at some length until, finally, somebody asked Dave if he had read the book.

"No, I haven't," he replied jokingly, "but I think what I'll do is to take a black marker and go through the book and mark out all the swear words first. Then I'll read it."

"Well, Dave," Auntie Kay piped up with that same little grin on her face, "you had better have lots of time to spare, because you're going to be awfully busy."

# Chapter 20: A Salute to a Schoolteacher

*"A golden throne is reserved in history for those, who in their time, choose to record history."*
—Brent Connelly, forester

Whenever I have the chance to give a talk to public library groups or school kids about some of my old logger friends, I take the opportunity to tell this good news story, hoping that a seed may fall on some fertile ground.

The story has special significance for me, because it involves a devoted schoolteacher interested in history. My own mother, Marion Connelly, had a similar interest in history and was also a devoted teacher who taught grade one students in Lachute and Brownsburg for three decades.

Our home was directly across the street from the school where she taught, and the whole family would come home each day for lunch. (The same school that I had to walk through blinding snowstorms to reach, while other kids were being bused.) By twelve-thirty, a half-dozen of her students would gather on our huge front verandah, ready to walk their beloved teacher back to school. It was a Norman Rockwell moment to see her heading back to school with a string of little kids holding each one of her hands.

In the summer of 2006, Heather and I were attending a book fair at the Argenteuil Regional Museum in Carillon, Quebec, when Heather picked up a local history book. It had been produced by a dedicated schoolteacher and her enthusiastic students from the Grenville Elementary School in Grenville, Quebec.

The book is entitled, *Links to our Heritage*, and tells the history of various families and individuals in the region around this charming little Lower Ottawa Valley community.

The teacher, Nancy Bennett, engaged her nine- and ten-year-old students to learn of and record the personal history of some of their ancestors. This is how the project began, as described by Nancy in her introduction:

> One unit of our Social Studies curriculum focuses on the history of our region approximately one hundred years ago. Our class was offered, as a resource document, a copy of the book which resulted from the transcribing of a taped interview with Mr. Richard Young. It records in a personalized form, the realities of the lifestyle in

> the local region some eighty five years ago. The enthusiasm of the students in this class while hearing these "tales" in this form was intriguing! They were thrilled to know the date of the depression and what salaries were like "back then." It was a delight to see their excitement! This was an example to be followed. I could not miss this opportunity,

The group decided on a standard format of questions to be asked of parents, grand- and great-grandparents. Interviews were conducted by the students, equipped with tape recorders, which in itself provided the children with a splendid opportunity to develop their own communication skills. Eventually, the project took on a life of its own, with parents and other members of the community pitching in to help out with input and financing. Another teacher at the school, Vera Young, took on a heavy support role in the tasks of transcribing and publishing.

I wish I could recall where I read a thought which comes to mind as I think about this wonderful achievement. I believe it was author Roy MacGregor who penned it, but I can't be absolutely certain: "Whenever a person passes on, a book is lost."

It seems to me that Nancy and her spirited students have taken that reflection to heart. Now, the shelves of local homes and public libraries in their communities will be forever graced with a homegrown record of the lives of the loved ones who preceded them. Good for them!

# Chapter 21: Harrington is a State of Mind

*"A visit to Harrington, Quebec, is a trip to Scotland, without having to pack a suitcase or renew a passport."*

—Kenneth MacTavish, banking executive and world traveller

Harrington, Quebec, is less than an hour's drive up the road from Dunany and is another back-home place that has a special spot in my heart. It is here that I once worked as a boy doing a man's job on the Rouge River log drive. It's also where Heather's family, the MacTavishes, originally homesteaded, with many of their descendants still living there. Some say that they settled there because the countryside mirrored the Scottish homeland, with its sweeping meadows, rolling hills, and clear streams. Its simple charm makes it a poet's paradise.

But the true magic of Harrington is in the people who live there. I'll try to characterize that statement by describing a recent visit that Heather and I made to the community in search of information that would eventually lead us to an important personal decision.

In August of 2004, our cottage on Clear Lake was destroyed by fire caused by a lightning strike. We were in the cottage at the time of the mishap and miraculously escaped uninjured with the clothes on our backs. Shortly afterwards, however, we were faced with the decision of whether or not to rebuild. We researched the matter over several months by talking to as many experts as we could. (As it turned out the final decision was not to rebuild.)

One of our stops was to Harrington on a cold, winter Sunday morning to seek the advice of Garry MacTavish, one of Heather's cousins. Garry is a warm, witty, and soft-spoken man in his early fifties, well known throughout Argenteuil County as a master builder of many permanent homes and cottages. At the time, he operated a construction business along with his two sons.

Sadly, only a few months before our visit, Garry's wife, Joan, had passed way. One of his sons, Scott, was living with him at the time; another son, Jeff, lived just down the road a few miles, as did two daughters, Donna and Tracey, and their families. Across the road lived Garry's brother, Reid, and down over a big hill in a pristine valley, his eighty-five-year-old father, Mike, lived by himself on the family farm, where he still presided over fifty head of beef cattle. And up and down the road, scattered over the beautiful landscape of the Harrington Valley, were the homes of cousins—lots of them.

Scott greeted us at the door with a big smile and with a big hug for Heather. He and his girlfriend, Sarah, were leaving soon for a game of shinny in Brownsburg. Garry was over at a neighbour's fixing something. We spent a pleasant hour until Garry came home telling stories and hearing the latest news, ranging from the newest babies to speculation about the latest marijuana plantation in the nearby hills of Avoca.

When asked if there was anybody growing weed in Harrington, Garry replied sternly, "Not a chance."

As we chatted, the phone rang steadily. First, it was Scott's brother with a reminder to be picked up for the hockey game in Brownsburg. There were also calls from friends, neighbours and his two daughters checking on what he was planning for Sunday dinner.

After I had filled about six pages of notes about the construction business, it was time to go for lunch and we were off to the centre of the Harrington universe, Campbell's Restaurant and Depanneur. On the way to the car, Garry gave me a baseball cap showing the logo of his construction business.

Over the years, I have discovered one thing about visiting MacTavishes in Harrington. Always be prepared to come away with a gift, either a bag of fresh buns, a chunk of venison, or a baseball cap. It's always something.

As we passed the little United Church, there were a few cars in the parking lot for the morning service and Garry identified the owners of most of the vehicles. "I hope they put in a good word for me," he said with a grin. "I don't know if they can cover it all in an hour service."

When we drove by Teddy Purcell's home, he filled us in on the near-miss incident that Teddy had a few weeks before when the snowplow truck he was driving caught fire and burned.

We could hardly find a parking space at Campbell's. The yard was full of skidoos, pickup trucks, and cars. Over to one side was a loaded log truck, and underneath, a couple of men doing some repairs. When we went into the restaurant, the greetings of "G'day, Garry," burst out from all directions. And then the buzz started with a steady stream of people dropping by our table for a visit. I jumped up out of my seat to shake hands with so many people that it took me over an hour to eat a single cheeseburger. A heaping plate of their steamy, mouth-watering poutine would have taken all afternoon to consume.

Then along came a carload of older, French-speaking people. They were hopelessly lost, and Garry asked them if he could help. An old guy stood by our table for at least five minutes mumbling in French about driving around in circles all morning. He didn't think that he would ever see home again. Garry drew them a map on a napkin and off they went sporting big smiles.

After lunch, we spotted another cousin, logger operator Charlie Downing, near the log truck. He was helping one

Mike MacTavish's farm, Harrington, Quebec.

of his truckers replace a drive shaft, and Charlie and I exchanged some bush talk as we stood out in the cold parking lot. I asked him how the logging business was, and he replied with his big trademark smile, "If I'm lucky this year, I'll just starve to death." Then he added with a more serious look on his face, "It sure doesn't get any easier. I can't install a simple culvert on a logging road anymore without getting a goddamned permit signed by the Queen."

When we were ready to leave to go home, Garry mentioned that he was going to visit his dad for the afternoon.

He added with a hint of guilt, "I haven't seen him all week. He loves visitors. Why don't you come along?"

From the top of the hill we looked down on a dazzling blanket of sparkling snow surrounding Mike's farmhouse and barns. The wood smoke from the chimney created the image of a single candle atop the middle of a giant white birthday cake after the guest-of-honour had made a successful wish. The snow was undisturbed except for some skidoo tracks on the side of a big hill in the distance and some coyote tracks leading to the barn. (Later, Mike explained without concern that there had been some calving activity in the barn and that the coyotes had come in search of the after-birth.)

It took a few minutes for Mike to answer the door. His rumpled, reddish hair and a blanket on a nearby couch were signs that he had been having an early afternoon nap. He told us that he had been out to the barn a couple of times during the night to assist with the newborns. A couple of huge flashlights on a windowsill and a pair of rubber boots placed neatly on a doormat provided evidence of that.

We were greeted with a huge smile and a hefty MacTavish handshake with a hand as big as a catcher's mitt. Heather got her tenth hug of the day.

Now it was storytelling time once again, as we sat down around the kitchen table. We went from mad cow disease to a blow-by-blow account of the new cement factory at Kilmar. Then came reams of MacTavish family history from an old-timer with a mind as sharp as somebody half his age.

Finally, it was time for us to leave for home. "But first, you will have to have a toddy with me," Mike insisted. Out of the cupboard came a bottle of Glenfiddich along with three waterglasses. Heather was instantly appointed by the group to be the designated driver for the trip back to Ottawa. The whisky was poured with a steady hand right out of the bottle. Not a jigger anywhere in sight, or even the suggestion of an ice cube or a little water to top it up.

When we left about an hour later, Garry stayed to visit more with his father. The scene: a father and son quietly chatting and sitting alone around a farmhouse kitchen table, until somebody else stopped by. And what did I say about having to take something with you at the end of a visit? We left with a huge roast of moose and three copies of *Cattlemen—The Beef Magazine*.

What an amazing day it had been!

It's with wonderment that I reflect on the gentle spirit covering that magnificent valley. You don't have to be a MacTavish or a local resident to sense it. Some might go to church in search of it. But all you really have to do is to jump into a vehicle with a friend on a Sunday afternoon and go visit somebody.

It's a spirit that has young people building houses and having babies just down the road from their parents and grandparents. Brothers pick up brothers to go play hockey. People lean on each other, and care and watch over friends, neighbours, and relatives. And on a quiet Sunday afternoon, faithful sons visit their aging fathers to chat, and maybe even have a moose steak supper together.

That is the magic of Harrington.

Charlie Downing, with help from his wife Pat, operates a logging business out of a garage beside the family home about a mile up the road from Garry's place. He owns skidders and road construction equipment and logs on various crown and private lands, and occasionally on his own deeded property. Charlie stands out in a crowd with his clear, rimmed glasses, bordering a rugged face and larger-than-life smile.

I first met Charlie on a Saturday night in 1997 at a MacTavish family reunion in the Harrington Community Centre. He and Garry were bellying up to the bar while my brother-in-law, Del MacTavish Jr., and I were standing nearby sipping on diet cokes and trying to decide which church service we would attend the following morning.

Mike MacTavish on his farm in Harrington, Quebec, "Where a little jigger is a newborn calf and not a shot glass."

Garry spotted us and came over to introduce Charlie. It wasn't long before we realized that we were brothers in the fraternity of loggers, and that's when the stories and the tall tales started. By the time we had finished logging that night, Charlie and I were ankle-deep in sawdust at one end of the dance floor.

When I told Charlie that I had worked as a sixteen-year-old boy in Harrington on the Rouge River log drive and in the bush for Canadian International Paper Company up the river, he said, "I know exactly where you worked. I'm logging in the same area now. How would you like to go for a ride back into the bush tomorrow morning for old-time's sake?" He didn't have to pass that by me twice. Del would have to find somebody else to go to church with.

We were staying in our motorhome that weekend behind the Community Centre up against a line fence adjoining a farmer's field. At 6:00 the next morning, I was awakened by a bawling steer as he peeked over the fence into our bedroom window, his wet nose nudging against the screen. Through the other open window came the rumble of Charlie's three-quarter-ton diesel truck, chugging away as Charlie waited for me to put on my pants and boots, and quickly grab an apple for breakfast.

As we drove into the bush, it wasn't long before I began to recognize some landmarks while we picked up with a carryover of stories from the night before. While he skilfully wheeled his truck along the narrow gravel roads, Charlie treated me to tales about some of the colourful characters he had worked with and known over the years.

Charlie Downing, logging operator, Harrington, Quebec: "My men work hard and smart in the bush. I'd like to see that Suzuki lad come up to the job some day in his big fancy bus wearing a fig leaf and a pair of Crocs. They'd teach him a few things about forest management."

At one time there were three or four Dougal MacLeans living in this country. To distinguish one from the other, locals tagged them with the name of the community that they came from. One logger, who was from the village of Fassett, was called "Fassett" Dougal MacLean. "Fassett" Dougal was in between jobs one spring and decided to visit the bright lights of Montreal. He caught the train to the city and painted up the town for a few days.

He was flat broke when it came time to return home, so he went to Windsor Station and sneaked onto the passenger train. He crouched down in a back seat hoping that the conductor would pass him by when collecting tickets. No such luck.

When the train stopped in St. Eustache, the conductor took him to the back of the train, kicked him in the arse and threw him off. But before the train had left the station "Fassett" Dougal sprinted to a front car and jumped on board once again. The conductor caught up to him for the second time, and when the train stopped at Lachute, Dougal was dragged to an open door and had his arse kicked off the train one more time.

As he stumbled around on the station platform trying to get back to his feet, the conductor yelled at him, "By the way, where in hell are you heading anyway?"

"I want to go to Fassett," replied a weary and sore Dougal, "if my arse can stand it."

That story reminded Charlie of another tale—one that had an anatomical connection.

A number of years ago there was a church tea on a Saturday afternoon just up the road in Avoca. And, as strange as it sounds, a group of loggers turned up. They must have heard that there was going to be a big lunch served. They gathered as a group in one corner of the hall and began chowing down the "sangwiches."

And what was the topic of their conversation? Logging, bulldozing, and trucking. But after awhile when they started to repeat the same tired yarns, they switched to their second most favourite subject—women.

As it turned out, a well-known floozie from the area was also at the tea. She had quite a reputation and was known by the boys as one who was inclined to pass herself around the country a bit.

One of the lads spotted her sitting at the opposite end of the hall and eagerly pointed her out to the group.

"By Jeez, you know," he whispered, "just last week, somebody told somebody that our lady over there is pregnant."

"Well, I'll be damned," another said, "I wonder if she knows who the father is."

Elmer Kelly, a quiet-spoken man, looked up from the piece of chocolate cake he was enjoying and, with a glint in his eye, offered softly, "What the hell does it matter? If you got slapped across the arse with a crosscut saw, would you know what tooth cut ya?"

One of the loggers who was at the tea that afternoon was Harry Young from Avoca. Harry had just returned from some kind of a bus tour around the countryside and he was telling his chums about the experience.

"Well, sir, we were jammed in like sardines in that damned bus. The driver was wearing glasses, and we were packed in so tight that there were six of us looking through them."

One winter, Charlie worked in the bush with a French lad named Jean-Pierre. He was a big man with a huge nose and he wore his hair long. He looked a little like Tiny Tim, and that's what everyone called him—Tiny.

Tiny came from a family of sixteen and was one of the most resourceful men Charlie had ever known. He guessed it came from scratching and clawing for the very basics of life back on the rock pile of a farm that he was raised on. If Tiny couldn't build or craft something, then he didn't need it. He was a master improviser and could make a gun holster out of a pig's ear.

They were logging for CIP up in St. Remi D'Amherst on a bitterly cold morning in January (as Charlie's father used to say, colder than a stepmother's breath). The men were all bundled up with parkas and scarves as they walked up a big hill to begin the day's work. Tiny was walking alongside Charlie, and when Charlie looked over at him, he could hardly believe his eyes. He wasn't wearing a hard hat liner. His hard hat sat perched on top of his bare head, and he was holding onto his ears with woolen mitts trying to keep them warm.

Finally, as Tiny's ears were starting to turn white with the frost, he stopped. He sat down on a nearby stump and rolled up one pant leg. He took a jackknife out of a pocket, pulled down the leg of his long underwear, and cut about four inches off the cuff. He removed his hard hat and pulled the piece of underwear down over his ears, stood up, and with a big smile, started walking back up the trail. Talk about giving new meaning to the term long johns.

Yes, sir, there was nothing going to keep old Tiny from going to the bush for a good day's work, even if one leg was four inches shorter than the other.

As Charlie said, "You guys up in Algoma may be able to talk about working with "Tilty" Tommy Tompkins at one time. But one very cold day many years ago on top of a big hill, we had our very own—"Tilty" Tiny Tim."

As we drove around Harrington that morning, Charlie and I chatted about some of the men I had worked with over forty years before. I mentioned Willie Diamond, and Charlie went on to tell me a story about Willie's dad, Kenny.

One Saturday afternoon, Kenny was hitchhiking down the Ridge Road in Harrington when he was picked up by a bunch of crazy young lads in an old car. They were on a bender and had a case of beer opened up on the front seat. And they were driving like fools. The old car rocked back and forth as it raced down the gravel road leaving a cloud of dust in its wake. It scared Kenny so bad that he asked them to let him out at the church corner.

When Kenny opened the door to get out of the car, he yelled back to the young idiots, "I don't know where you lads are going, but it ain't going to take you too long to get there."

I asked Charlie about Howard "Please and Thanks" MacLean, and, of course, he had a story to tell me about him. Howard was nicknamed "Please and Thanks" because whenever he told you something or asked a question, he would add a please and thanks. That was his trademark. He had a farm near the Rouge River, and, like a lot of farmers in those days, used to work in the bush during the winter. I had worked with him on the log drive.

Charlie described an incident that happened one winter day when Howard and Ernie McLeod were loading logs onto sleighs with a horse jammer. (There are many variations to the use of a jammer. A conventional jammer was a tripod-like structure on wooden skids made from logs and equipped with cables and pulleys. Depending on the size of the timber and the loading conditions, a single horse or a team of horses was used to load the logs. A cable was connected to each end of a log by a hook which was driven into the log. These hooks were called pig's feet and were secured by a man working at each end of the log. The cable was fed up through a pulley at the top of the tripod and attached by a chain to the horse's whippletree. As the teamster led the horses away from the sleigh, the log was raised onto the sleigh where a top loader placed it in a safe position on the load with a cant hook.)

Ernie McLeod was well-known throughout the country as an expert teamster. His horses were always in top condition, and he was very proud of them. However, Ernie had not always been a logger. As a younger man, he worked at the magnesite mine in Kilmar, where unfortunately he lost an eye in a grinding accident and had to be fitted with a glass eye.

On this particular day, instead of the conventional method of loading sawlogs with pig's feet, Howard was using a single set of tongs to load large four-foot hardwood pulpwood, which he hooked around the middle of the block.

As they were loading one piece, Ernie and Howard apparently got their signals crossed, and Ernie's horses took off before Howard had the tongs properly set. The tongs slipped and caught the end of Howard's pant leg, tearing the pants right off him. And there he was, standing in the middle of the bush on a cold winter's day, somewhere "inbacka" Harrington . . . pantless.

"I was lucky," Howard explained afterwards. "I only ended up with a scratch or two, please and thanks, but that one-eyed scissorbill of an Ernie must have had his good eye on his golled-darned horses and the glass one on me . . ."

Unlike today, where cut and skid crews pre-cut the road right-of-way before bulldozing and forming begins, back in those days, the dozers pushed over the trees themselves. Emile Laurin was a dozer operator for CIP at one time. His helper, Clarence MacMahon, used a chainsaw to limb and cut the fallen trees into log lengths. Clarence told of a near miss he once had when he and Emile were building some new logging roads north of Harrington.

"Emile pushed down a big brute of a yellow birch tree, and it landed up against a huge stone. It had a pretty good bow to it, and I was a little bit afeered to cut the top off it in case it would spring back on me. I sized it up pretty good and began to cut slowly. Suddenly, a limb snapped and the top of the tree shot back and struck me right on the side of my foot.

"By the holy old jumpins, that frigging ankle swelled up quicker than a horny hen could flag down a rooster. I had just bought a new pair of boots a few days before and couldn't put one on because of the swelling. So, for the next two weeks, I walked around in the box that they came in."

It was then that the discussion about logging accidents turned serious, as Charlie and I shared some of the horrors that we had both experienced in the bush. Words cannot describe the sinking feeling when seeing a man running out of the bush, waving his arms to signal a chum injured and down under a fallen tree or large branch at the top of a big hill. And all too often, the site would be miles and perhaps hours away from medical help.

Charlie told of one day when Garry was driving with him in the bush. He was telling Garry of his concern about how all the men were travelling in pickup trucks making it very difficult to carry a stretcher around on the job.

It was at that point that Charlie pulled the truck over to the side of the road, stopped, and said, "I have something to show you." He reached in behind the seat of the truck and pulled out a large bag. "Can you believe this?" he asked. "A month or so after the day Garry and I were out in the bush, he showed up at my place one night and gave this to me."

It was a handmade, fold-up, hardwood stretcher with four sturdy handles that Garry had cleverly crafted himself. Small enough to fold up and fit behind the seat of a truck—large and durable enough to carry a 250-pound logger.

There lies more of the magic of that special place, with one of its sons thinking that the next man to be carried out of the bush might be a cousin, a good friend, or just somebody who lived up the road. He was going to do all he could to make sure an injured logger would be safely transferred to medical assistance.

And for the rest of us, a glimpse at another miracle of life: No matter what the circumstances are or wherever we choose to look, goodness is never very far out of sight.

Goodness is everywhere in our lives. And, yes, it can even be found behind the seat of Charlie Downing's pickup truck.

# Epilogue

I'll wind up this little glimpse into my past with some brief commentary about three important dynamics that I have been witness to over the last forty years of working in forestry. Firstly, there is the evolving, progressive change in forest management practices, and, for two long decades, its unsettling effect on the forest industry. Secondly, there is the forest itself and the endless varieties of flora and fauna that it nurtures. And finally, and most importantly for me now as I reflect on some of the wonderful people I have worked with during that time, there are the people who work in it.

When I left Algonquin Park to work in Algoma in 1965, the forest management controls were in the form of minimum stump diameters. Only trees over a certain size could be harvested, and because there were limited markets for low-quality timber products at that time, only the best trees were taken. It was a filet mignon diet—the hamburger was left behind still standing, putting the forest in a sharp state of decline.

However, within ten short years the diet began to change. The steak was then being left on the stump to form the upgraded forest of the future.

Several factors were at play: lower-quality trees were being designated for harvest with paint by trained forest technicians; pulpwood market conditions began to improve slightly; and some lumber companies began the costly process of re-tooling their mills to match the supply of lower quality timber.

And that presents me with an opportunity to extend a tip of the hat to the small three-, four-, and five-generation family lumber companies who have been the lifeline of their communities for decades as they stuck it out during a very difficult transition period. They had their family pride and the survival of their communities at stake. They weren't going anywhere no matter how tough things became. Besides, they had vision enough to recognize the long-term benefits of a well-managed forest.

So while the big boys like Weyerhaeuser and Weldwood had bailed out and were on their way to greener side-hills, small family firms such as McRae Lumber Co. of Whitney and Murray Bros. Lumber of Madawaska were putting everything on the line with major investments to modify their mills.

Good for them . . . and let us all hope that their faith in the future will stand tall in the eyes of the public policy-makers as they contemplate changes in land-use zoning in Algonquin Park that would adversely affect the regional forest industry.

I was there on the eve of the termination of logging in Lake Superior Park, and it wasn't pretty. It affected my family and many others. All one has to do to gain an appreciation for the consequences of such a decision is visit the site of the once proud Weyerhaeuser mill complex in Sault Ste. Marie where an old sawmill still gasps for breath. The many derelict and abandoned restaurants, gas stations, and homes along Highway 17 between the Soo and Wawa are also stark reminders of good times long past.

The forests of Algonquin Park have never, in the history of the park, been in as good shape or better managed than they are now. That needs to continue, as do the livelihoods of the many hard-working people who depend on forestry operations in Algonquin to feed their babies and pay their mortgages.

Every moment of every day there is change in the life of a forest.

While seasons change, tiny seeds of life germinate into tree seedlings; juvenile trees compete with each other in a valiant effort to reach for the freedom of the sky; mature trees stand proudly protecting the understorey of new growth; and finally, the aging members of the family that tower over all the others struggle to fight off disease and the inevitability of death.

On my brief pass through, I have seen new stands of trees forming and old trees succumbing to time and the occasional destructive servings of Mother Nature, and yes, even some abuse by man. Generations of moose, deer, beaver, turtles, and hawks have come and faded away. Nothing stands still in the forest. It is forever alive with newness and the passing on.

Like the trees and the animals, the men who work in the bush arrive for their time there, and they too must move on. This was never better highlighted to me than on the drive across Canada I mentioned earlier.

It was a cold, rainy morning in early June, as Heather and I drove north from Sault Ste. Marie on Highway 17. As we passed Batchawana Bay, dense fog prevented us from seeing the beauty of Lake Superior which was only a couple of hundred feet from the edge of the highway. Rain pounded the windshield as we neared the turn off into the old Mile 67 camp site, which was a quarter of a mile from the highway. I sensed a feeling of nostalgia upon deciding to see what the site looked like now, thirty-two years after I had left it. Weyerhaeuser had removed the camps many years before, and I had been told that the site had been rehabilitated and returned to its natural state.

Our car became a time capsule as I rounded the turn, looking for something recognizable, expecting only to see dense bush where the camp had once stood. I couldn't believe my eyes as I stared in amazement at another one of those logger's mirages that they talk about in the bunkhouse after supper. There, in exactly the same location as the camp I had stayed in, was a different set of logging camps.

There were several portable crew trailers set up where the old bunkhouse and cookery had once been. A front-end loader was parked nearby, along with a couple of pickup trucks, one of them displaying the logo of Avery Construction Ltd. of Sault Ste. Marie. (I learned later that this was the logging contractor now working in the Mile 67 area to supply logs to the former Weyerhaeuser sawmill in the Soo.)

As we pulled up in front of the open door of one of the trailers, I spotted a lonely figure straddling a chair, smoking a cigarette, and peering out at the rain from inside the cookery trailer. He stood up as we approached, and when I jumped up on the step of the trailer to speak to him, he blurted out with a surprised look on his face, "Brent Connelly, you old bugger! Is that you or is that your ghost?"

That was my second surprise of the day. The best was yet to come, however, because as soon as I saw his smile and the twinkle in his eyes, I also knew who he was—old friend, Rolly Goodfellow. Now in his early sixties, Rolly was one of the bush mechanics I had once worked with at Mile 100 and Mile 67.

And how were we able to recognize each other after more than three decades? Well, it has been said that old loggers never really change—they just keep adding annual rings and girth, causing the bark to become a little more gnarly and furrowed.

The last time I saw Rolly, he was a skinny, curly-haired young guy wearing oily coveralls with an oblong "Rolly" identity patch on his chest and a grease rag hanging out of a back pocket. One hand was never without

A new generation of loggers with a couple of old-timers passing over the torch, Mile 67, Algoma: Darcy Agawa, Rolly Goodfellow, Craig Corbett, Brent Connelly, Steve Farkas.

a wrench, and the side of his mouth always held a weary-looking cigarette, bearing trademark black finger smudges from hands well used to twisting on hydraulic hoses and cranking on ratchet wrenches.

The curly hair was still all there, only now it had taken on a salt-and-pepper hue. There were a few more pounds, but not too many. The cigarette hadn't moved and was still smudged, evidence that Rolly was still working as a bush mechanic.

There were three other men in the cookery sitting at a table having a quick cup of coffee. They wouldn't be there long because, even though it was raining hard and too wet to go to the logging site, they had other work to do. Perhaps a chainsaw had to be tuned up or a worn-out skidder tire changed. Maybe they would take a trip to town for parts.

And that is when it hit me. These were all young men in their twenties and early thirties. I was looking at the next generation of loggers, and they were an impressive looking group. They were lean and muscular with only the slightest possibility of a pot-belly still decades down the road. As we chatted briefly, I sensed a professionalism and a pride in their work. These men would not be content confined to an office or factory. Instead, they were well-trained free spirits who preferred a physically challenging and rewarding outdoor life working in the forests of Algoma.

It was out with the old for Rolly and me. But it was in with the new, as proven by these fine young men who were now logging in the same Negick and Bow Lake area that Tony Vorlicek and I had first pioneered in the 1960s.

It is my hope that before their generation ends and the next one takes over harvesting timber at Mile 67, some old storyteller will sit down and tell their tales.

And the thought of that makes me feel finer than the hair on the little frog that is relaxing on the front cover of this book!

# References

*The Eganville Leader*, May 24, 2006.

Anderson, Mark. *Ottawa Citizen*, Dec 13, 2006.

Bateman, Janice Connelly. McVicar/MacVicar Family Tree. November 2004.

Connelly, Brent. *Holy Old Whistlin'—Yarns About Algonquin Park Loggers.* (Renfrew: GSPH) 2005.

Montgomery, E. M. (Red). Ontario Department Of Lands and Forests, internal memo, dated October 30, 1969.

Morrison, Willis Nelson. *From Horse and Buggy to Jet Age—A Story of the Morrison Family During the 1900s.*

Townsend, E. R. *Algonquin Forestry Authority—A 20 year History, 1975–1995.*

www.Weyerhaeuser.com

http://en.wikipedia.org/wiki/Dowsing

*Farmers Supply Company - 50 years of service*

*Links to our Heritage - Level 3/4 Grenville Elementary School—1999.*

**Photo credits:**

- Tony Vorlicek
- Paul Nenonen
- Roy Perkins
- Ray and Lynda Harnish
- Duncan, Mark, and Michelle Jamieson
- Bob Pick
- Jeff Driscoll
- Arnold Johnston
- Harvey Rutz
- John and Heather Fox
- Ernest Morrison
- Barbara Fodor
- Tom Cameron
- Emily and Carlie Harnish
- Jack Schreader

# About the Author

Brent Connelly was raised in Brownsburg, Quebec, a small hillside town nestled on the edge of the Lower Ottawa Valley and the Laurentian Mountains. In 1961, he obtained a Bachelor of Science degree in Forestry and went on to enjoy a fulfilling career in forestry which spanned four decades. During that time, he worked in the forests of Ontario's two premier provincial parks, Algonquin and Lake Superior.

Brent was employed by McRae Lumber Co. Ltd. of Whitney, Ontario, Weyerhaeuser Canada Ltd. in Sault Ste. Marie and Mattawa, Ontario, and the Algonquin Forestry Authority in Pembroke, Ontario. His retirement came in 2000 after twenty-five years with the AFA.

Brent and Heather, his wife of thirty-nine years, now live in Ottawa. They have seven children and eleven grandchildren.

Brent Connelly is also the author of *Holy Old Whistlin'—Yarns About Algonquin Park Loggers*, which was published by General Store Publishing House in 2005.

# To Order More Copies of:

*Contact:*